About the Author

Jithin Aby Alex, CISSP, CEH

Security Professional, having experience in implementing and handling major network security solutions and products in various environments and regions. I have used my experience, professional connection and publicly available information for writing this book. Personally I thank you for purchasing this book and thanks for the support. I hope this book will be informative to you and I wish you all the best.

Please visit www.jaacostan.com for my articles and technical write-ups.

Copyright © Jithin Aby Alex

"The expert in everything was once a beginner."

Table of Contents

Introduction

Cisco's firewall road-map has been interesting. They started with PIX and advanced the firewall security market with ASA. After acquiring Sourcefire, they came up with Firepower services. Firepower services on ASA was offering a lot of security features and has helped to fill the feature gaps within ASA, but it was running as two separate instances. That is ASA and Firepower.

Cisco has come up with Firepower Threat Defense (FTD), which is a unified image of ASA and Firepower. It is designed to do what ASA and what Firepower can, together with unified management. Cisco FTD is capable of offering traditional ASA services plus NGIPS features, URL Filtering, Application visibility and control (AVC), Advance Malware Protection, ISE Integration, SSL Decryption, Captive Portal, Multi-Domain Management and other optimizations in application visibility and access control etc.

Managing Cisco FTD has also been changed with the introduction of the new tool called as Firepower Device Manager (FDM), which is a replacement for ASDM and the centralized Firepower Management Center. This book will cover both Cisco FTD and FMC, its integration, configuration and management in detail.

Cisco is now focusing more on FTD and eventually the traditional ASA OS might get retired. So those who are used to ASA firewalls and those who are trying to learn firewalls should keep this in mind and should learn to configure and manage Cisco FTD. This book is for you and I have explained all the necessary things in detail with illustrations.

How to use this book?

This book is written like a learning course, explained in detail with a lab topology using FTDv. Hence this is a 100% practical guide on configuring and managing Cisco Firepower Threat Defense Next Generation Firewall using Cisco Firepower Management Center. I have also covered the standalone firewall introduction and how to use Firepower Device Manager to manage your FTD firewall locally without using FMC. The learning flow of this book is as follows,

- Understand the lab topology.
- Install Cisco FTD.
- Install and configure Cisco FMC.
- Integrate Cisco FTD with FMC.
- Configure and manage Cisco FTD using FMC.
- Upgrade Cisco ASA to FTD.
- Configure and manage Cisco FTD using local manager, which is the Firepower Device Manager (FDM).
- Introduction to the Cisco FTD migration tool.

This book doesn't cover the topics such as VPN, SGT, and Cisco ISE integration. All other major concepts and options are explained in this book.

Pre-requisites

Basic understanding of networking protocols and devices. CCNA level networking knowledge. Prior understanding of Cisco ASA firewall is a good for fast learning but not mandatory. If you are not using physical appliances, then knowledge on GNS3 is preferred for setting up the lab.

What is Cisco FTD?

As mentioned in the introduction, Cisco Firepower Threat Defense (FTD) is a unified software image, which includes the Cisco ASA features and Firepower Services. This unified software is capable of offering the function of ASA and Firepower in one platform, both in terms of hardware and software features. Cisco FTD is available as both virtual and appliance. The virtual version is represented as FTDv. When it comes to appliances, the 2100, 4100 and 9300 series are a whole new hardware platform for security appliances based on the UCS hardware. They offer much higher performance when compared to the ASA platforms.

 The Cisco Firepower Threat Defense (FTD) is capable of offering following Next-Generation Firewall Services

- Stateful firewall Capabilities
- Static and dynamic routing
- Supports RIP, OSPF, BGP, Static Routing but not EIGRP.
- Next-Generation Intrusion Prevention Systems (NGIPS)
- URL Filtering
- Application visibility and control (AVC)
- Advance Malware Protection (AMP)
- ISE Integration
- SSL Decryption
- Captive Portal
- Multi-Domain Management

Currently Cisco Firepower Threat Defense (FTD) unified software can be deployed on Cisco Firepower 2100, 4100 Series and the Firepower 9300 appliances as well the FTD can be also be deployed on Cisco Firepower Threat Defense (FTD) ASA 5506-X, ASA 5506H-X, ASA 5506W-X, ASA5508-X, ASA 5512-X, ASA 5515-X, ASA 5516-X, ASA 5525-X, ASA 5545-X, and ASA 5555-X. However, the Cisco Firepower Threat Defense (FTD) unified software cannot be deployed on Cisco ASA 5505 and 5585-X Series appliances.

Also note that, as of now Multi Context mode, EIGRP and Multicast is not supported by FTD.

Datasheet   **from**   **Cisco**:
https://www.cisco.com/c/en/us/products/collateral/security/firepower-ngfw/datasheet-c78-736661.html

Lab Topology

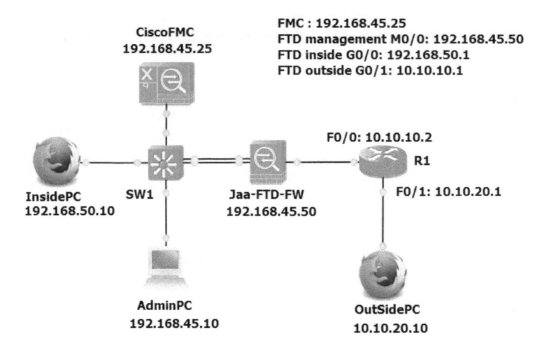

Item	Description
Cisco FTDv	Cisco Firepower Threat Defense for KVM (75) Version 6.2.0 (Build 363)
Cisco FMCv	Cisco Firepower Management Center for KVM v6.2.0 (build 362
Tiny Linux Firefox Appliance	Two Tiny Linux appliances. One act as the inside user and the other as Outside user
Cisco C2961 router	Outside zone router
Generic L2 switch	Acting as a connection point between devices.

The above topology is used for explaining the concepts and connectivity. I have used the virtual versions of Cisco FMC and FTD, and as the platform I have used GNS3. You may set up a similar lab as physical or virtual, as per your convenience. Since I have explained everything with screenshots, reading this book will give you a broad understanding but I strongly recommend you to setup the lab and do practice.

Router configuration

Configure the interface IP addressing on the router for the basic connectivity. The router interface connected with the outside zone of firewall is FastEthernet 0/0 and is assigned with the IP address 10.10.10.2/24.

Another interface FastEthernet 0/1 is assigned with an IP address 10.10.20.1/24.

R1(config)#int fa0/0
R1(config-if)#ip add 10.10.10.2 255.255.255.0
R1(config-if)#no sh
R1(config-if)#

R1(config-if)#int fa0/1
R1(config-if)#ip add 10.10.20.1 255.255.255.0
R1(config-if)#no sh

I am accessing the Cisco FMC and FTD Console from the Admin PC, which is assigned with IP address 192.168.45.10. I have an inside user named as InsidePC with IP address 192.168.50.10.

Lab topology for High Availability.

There is a slight change in topology while configuring FTD devices in HA. I will be explaining the configuration in the **Configuring High Availability** chapter in the later section.

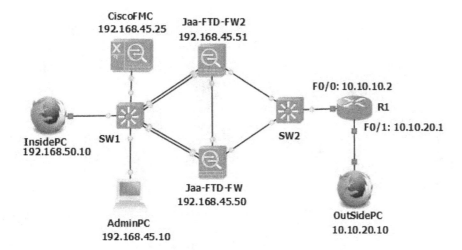

Setting up Cisco Firepower Threat Defense (FTD) Firewall

Once you powered on the Cisco FTD device, access the terminal using console.

When the device is boots up, it will prompt to enter the username and password. The default username is admin and password is Admin123

```
Cisco Firepower Threat Defense for KVM v6.2.0 (build 363)
firepower login: admin
Password: _
```

After successful login, you need to accept the EULA (License Agreement).

```
firepower login: admin
Password:
You must accept the EULA to continue.
Press <ENTER> to display the EULA: _
```

```
For all countries referred to above, the parties specifically disclaim the
application of the UN Convention on Contracts for the International Sale of
Goods.  Notwithstanding the foregoing, either party may seek interim
injunctive relief in any court of appropriate jurisdiction with respect to any
alleged breach of such party's intellectual property or proprietary rights.
If any portion hereof is found to be void or unenforceable, the remaining
provisions of the Agreement and Warranties shall remain in full force and
effect.  Except as expressly provided herein, the Agreement constitutes the
entire agreement between the parties with respect to the license of the
Software and Documentation and supersedes any conflicting or additional terms
contained in any Purchase Order or elsewhere, all of which terms are excluded.
The Agreement has been written in the English language, and the parties agree
that the English version will govern.

Product warranty terms and other information applicable to Cisco products are
available at the following URL: http://www.cisco.com/go/warranty.

Please enter 'YES' or press <ENTER> to AGREE to the EULA:  YES
```

You need to press enter to accept the EULA at the endo of the license statement.
After accepting the licensing agreement, then it's the time to configure the Network details for the management interface.

```
Please enter 'YES' or press <ENTER> to AGREE to the EULA:

System initialization in progress.  Please stand by.
You must change the password for 'admin' to continue.
Enter new password:
Confirm new password:
You must configure the network to continue.
You must configure at least one of IPv4 or IPv6.
Do you want to configure IPv4? (y/n) [y]:
Do you want to configure IPv6? (y/n) [n]:
Configure IPv4 via DHCP or manually? (dhcp/manual) [manual]:
Enter an IPv4 address for the management interface [192.168.45.45]: _
```

First change the default password. Then you need to provide the IP address details. As per my lab topology, I am using 192.168.45.50 as my management IP address. You can configure the IP address here. But here I am putting the default IP as it is. I will show you how to change the management IP, and at that point, I will assign 192.168.45.50.

```
System initialization in progress.  Please stand by.
You must change the password for 'admin' to continue.
Enter new password:
Confirm new password:
You must configure the network to continue.
You must configure at least one of IPv4 or IPv6.
Do you want to configure IPv4? (y/n) [y]:
Do you want to configure IPv6? (y/n) [n]: n
Configure IPv4 via DHCP or manually? (dhcp/manual) [manual]:
Enter an IPv4 address for the management interface [192.168.45.45]:
Enter an IPv4 netmask for the management interface [255.255.255.0]:
Enter the IPv4 default gateway for the management interface [192.168.45.1]:
Enter a fully qualified hostname for this system [firepower]:
Enter a comma-separated list of DNS servers or 'none' []:
Enter a comma-separated list of DNS servers or 'none' []: none
Enter a comma-separated list of search domains or 'none' []: none
If your networking information has changed, you will need to reconnect.
_
```

After providing the IP address details, you may type in the fully qualified name for your firewall and DNS details.

```
Configure firewall mode? (routed/transparent) [routed]:
Configuring firewall mode ...
```

Then it will prompt you about the firewall mode. Like in ASA, you have the same two options. Router or Transparent. Select the routed mode.

Then the firewall will perform the necessary processed for becoming the routed mode firewall.

```
Update policy deployment information
    - add device configuration
    - add network discovery
    - add system policy

You can register the sensor to a Firepower Management Center and use the
Firepower Management Center to manage it. Note that registering the sensor
to a Firepower Management Center disables on-sensor Firepower Services
management capabilities.

When registering the sensor to a Firepower Management Center, a unique
alphanumeric registration key is always required.  In most cases, to register
a sensor to a Firepower Management Center, you must provide the hostname or
the IP address along with the registration key.
'configure manager add [hostname | ip address ] [registration key ]'

However, if the sensor and the Firepower Management Center are separated by a
NAT device, you must enter a unique NAT ID, along with the unique registration
key.
'configure manager add DONTRESOLVE [registration key ] [ NAT ID ]'

Later, using the web interface on the Firepower Management Center, you must
use the same registration key and, if necessary, the same NAT ID when you add
this sensor to the Firepower Management Center.
> _
```

It may take few minutes and when the process is finished, you will get a ' >' prompt, which means the basic setup of Cisco FTD has been successfully done.

Note: If you are using FTDv, then there will be some slight differences on the CLI command options. The physical FTD is almost as some of the traditional Cisco ASA firewall. But the virtual version, that is the FTDv has some limitations on local management. You will miss commands like **enable, config terminal** etc on FTDv, as it is meant to be managed using a Cisco Firepower Management Center.

Changing Management IP

If you want to change the management IP details, then you may follow the command below.

Syntax:

> configure network ipv4 manual ip_address net_mast gateway interface_name

```
>configure network ipv4 manual 192.168.45.50 255.255.255.0
192.158.45.1
```

Interface name is not mandatory in FTDv.

```
> configure network ipv4 manual 192.168.45.50 255.255.255.0 192.168.45.1
Setting IPv4 network configuration.
Network settings changed.

>
```

If you are using a physical appliance, you may enter the command with the interface name.

```
> configure network ipv4 manual 192.168.45.50 255.255.255.0 192.168.45.1 Managem
ent0
Setting IPv4 network configuration.
Network settings changed.

> _
```

Once you configured the IP, you may verify it with **show network** command.

```
================[ System Information ]================
Hostname                 : firepower
Management port          : 8305
IPv4 Default route
  Gateway                : 192.168.45.1

====================[ eth0 ]====================
State                    : Enabled
Channels                 : Management & Events
Mode                     : Non-Autonegotiation
MDI/MDIX                 : Auto/MDIX
MTU                      : 1500
MAC Address              : 0C:D7:D8:73:54:00
------------------[ IPv4 ]------------------
Configuration            : Manual
Address                  : 192.168.45.50
Netmask                  : 255.255.255.0
Broadcast                : 192.168.45.255
------------------[ IPv6 ]------------------
Configuration            : Disabled

================[ Proxy Information ]================
State                    : Disabled
Authentication           : Disabled
--More--
```

Right. We have the Cisco FTD configured with a management IP and is ready to integrate with Cisco Firepower Management Center (FMC). TO manage the FTD, there are couple of options. One is manage locally using Cisco Firepower Device Manager, which is similar to ASDM. And the second option is manage the FTD using FMC. In this lab, we are managing the FTD using FMC.

Configure Manager in Cisco FTD.

Let's add the FMC as the manager on FTD.

```
> configure manager add 192.168.45.25 123456
```

Where 123456 is the secret key that I have used. You need this key for registering FTD with FMC.

```
> configure manager add 192.168.45.25 123456
```

Once added, you can verify using **show managers** command.

Well that is all the necessary basic setup needed on the Cisco FTD firewall. Now we need to add the FTD device in to FMC. Prior to that, let's setup and configure Cisco Firepower Management Center (FMC).

Setting up Cisco Firepower Management Center (FMC)

Boot up the Cisco Firepower Management Center server and once the booting is finished, you can see a prompt like this. Login using the default username **admin** and password **Admin123**

```
Cisco Firepower Management Center for KVM v6.2.0 (build 362)
firepower login: admin
Password:
Last login: Wed Oct  3 23:24:46 UTC 2018 on ttyS0

Copyright 2004-2017, Cisco and/or its affiliates. All rights reserved.
Cisco is a registered trademark of Cisco Systems, Inc.
All other trademarks are property of their respective owners.

Cisco Fire Linux OS v6.2.0 (build 42)
Cisco Firepower Management Center for KVM v6.2.0 (build 362)

admin@firepower:~$ █
```

There is nothing much to do on FMC CLI. Everything will be configured using the GUI interface of FMC. The default management IP is 192.168.45.45. Access the GUI using a web browser. https://192.168.45.45

Login using the default username and password. After login, you will be prompt to change your password and other settings such as IP address, adding license etc.

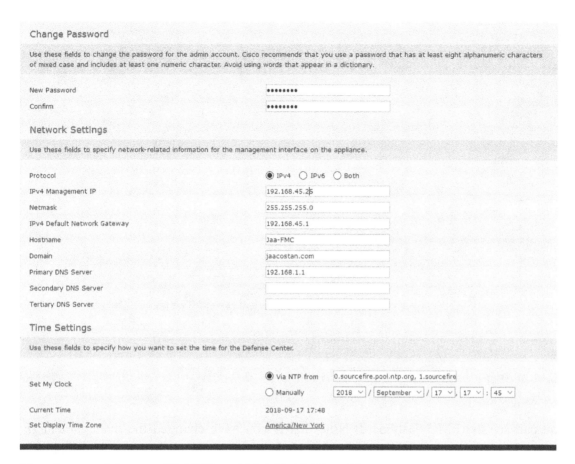

Here I entered the new FMC IP as 192.168.45.25 and hostname.

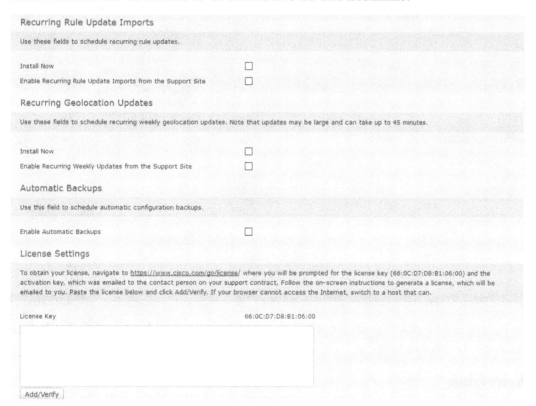

Enter the license key and verify. You can skip this step here by not giving a license key. Later you can fill the license details. Then accept the license agreements and click apply.

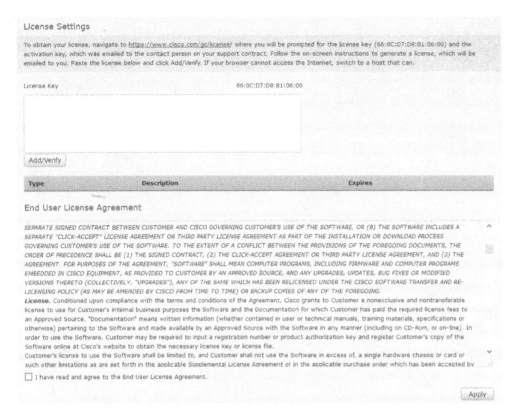

Now you can see the FMC dashboard. Note that if you have changed the management IP, then you need to access the FMC using the new IP. In my case, access **https://192.168.45.25**

I will be explaining the major tabs and options in the FMC graphical interface. But before that, I will activate the license here.

License Activation

To activate the license, go to **System -> Licenses -> Smart Licenses**

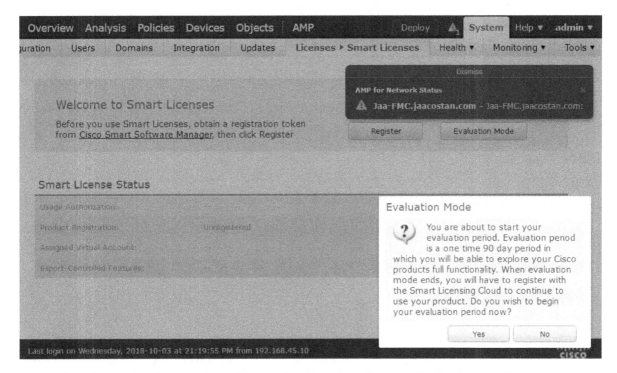

I am using the evaluation mode and for activating that click on Evaluation mode.

Once the evaluation mode is activated, you can explore and use the FMC for managing the cisco FTD devices in your infrastructure. The evaluation period is for 90 days. You can purchase a new license at the end of evaluation period.

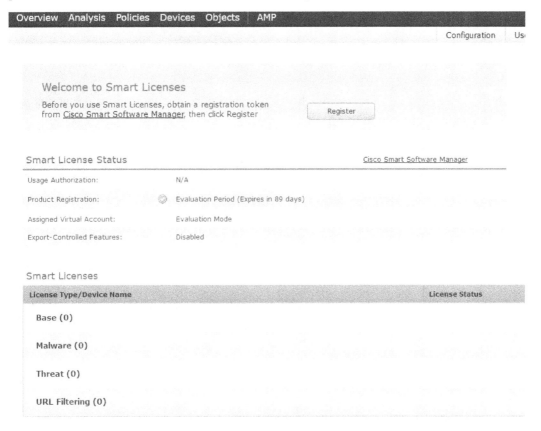

Once the license is activated, you can see the four license types in the license page. The four different licenses are,

1) Base: This is the base license that enables the basic Firewall features.

The remaining 3 are advanced licenses that are required for enabling the Next Generation firewall features.

2) Malware

3) Threat

4) URL filtering

Note that in order to activate the license, you should have a Smart licensing account and the FMC requires internet connectivity.

Explore the Cisco FMC options.

In this section, I am going to explain all the major options and tabs in the Cisco FMC graphical interface. You can see the major tabs such as Overview, Analysis, Policies, Devices, Objects and AMP. Each of them having multiple sub-options.

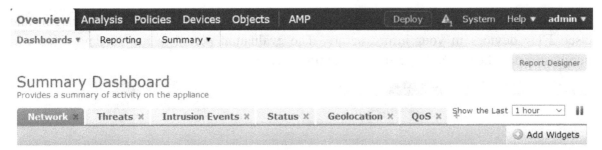

Let's start with the Overview tab. Overview shows the summary of the devices, its status and health. You can also view and generate reports as per the criteria you put.

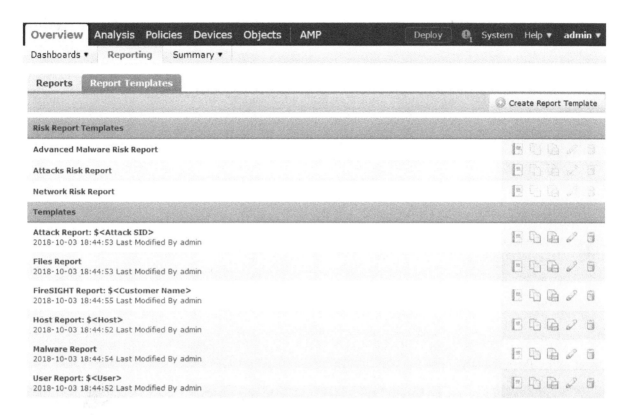

You can create a report template and generate it. Once the report is generated, it will be accessible on the Reports page.

You can also view the summary of incidents and events for each devices in your FMC, such as intrusion events, performance statistics etc.

Next is the Analysis Tab.

The Analysis page shows the most of Next Generation features. You can view all the events with all the security check details such as Intrusion attempts, what file, which user and what vulnerability. With all these information, you can able to get a full idea of a particular incident.

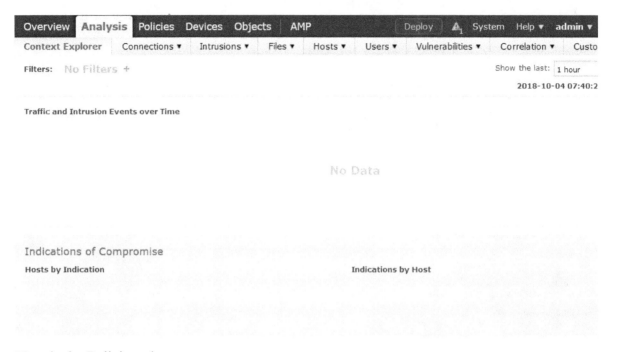

Next is the Policies tab,

There are 7 basic Access control policies. They are, Access Control, Intrusion, Malware & File, DNS, Identity, SSL and prefilter.

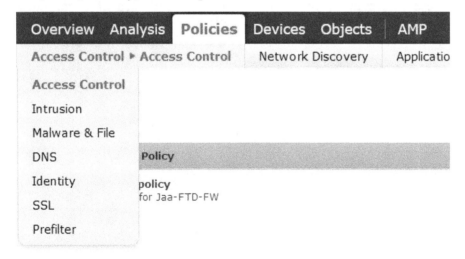

Normal access control rules will be created under the Access Control option.

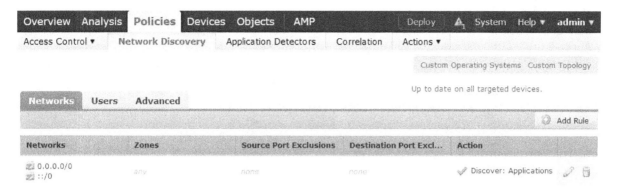

The Network Discovery tab shows all the discovered network associated with each of the FTD devices configured in the FMC.

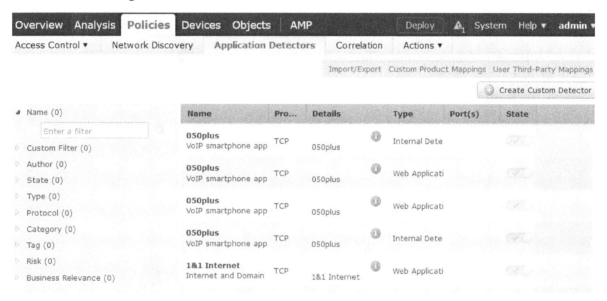

Application detectors shows the rules for detecting the applications used in the network. By default, FMC shows many application detectors. You can update or add new custom detectors in this section. These attributes will be used while creating an Access rule.

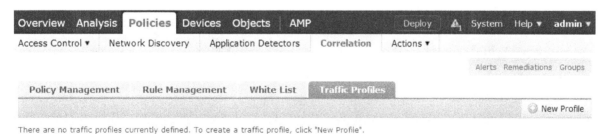

Correlation policy is used to take action for an event or a series of event. You can whitelist or can do further analysis on a particular event.

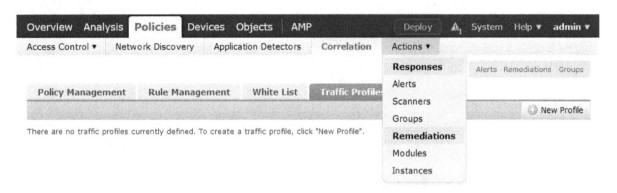

In the Action tab, you can view alerts and can create alert criteria. Also you can do an Nmap scan on a particular device using Scanners options. Also can specify remediation option for a particular incident or alert.

Next is the Devices tab,

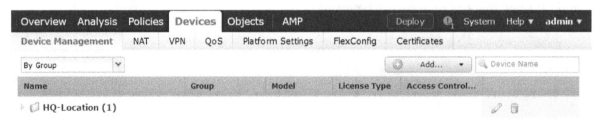

In this tab, you can view and add the FTD devices in to the FMC and can configure the NAT, VPN, QoS and other device settings.

You can create platform policies for the firepower devices from the platform settings tab. Platform settings include banner, security compliances and system related settings.

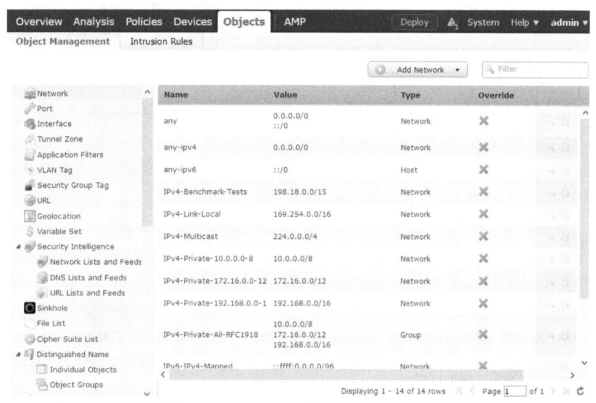

Objects tab has all the object details including the network, hosts, port, service, zones, URLs etc. You can create new objects under this tab. You can also view all the intrusion rules available under this tab.

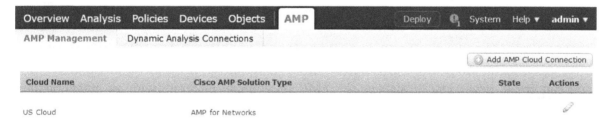

AMP stands for Anti Malware Protection and it need to connect with the AMP cloud to update and analyze the signatures and patterns.

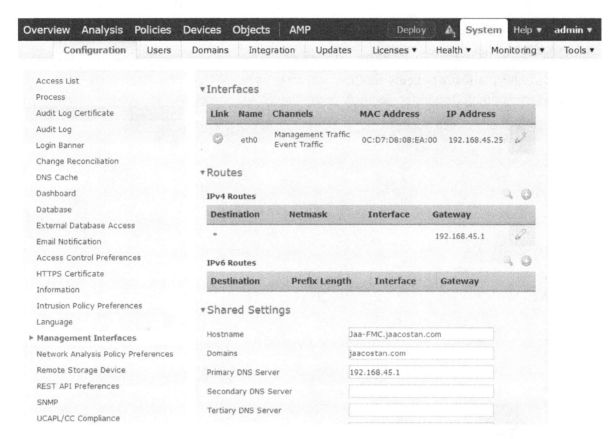

Under System tab, you can view and edit all the settings related to the FMC device. You can change the management IP, add login banners, logs, certificate, notifications etc under System-> Configuration option.

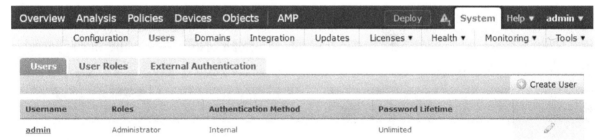

You can create new users to manage the FMC or you can integrate with an authentication server.

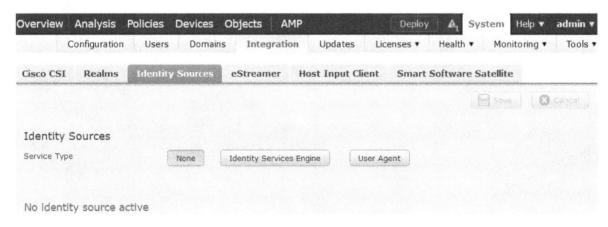

The FMC can be further integrated with other products and solutions such as Cisco Identity Services Engine (ISE), Cisco CSI, and Cisco Smart Software Manager etc.

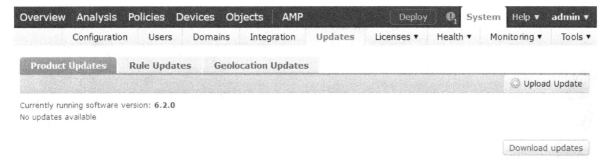

You can downloads the updates for the FMC and FTD, the rule updates from the Updates tab.

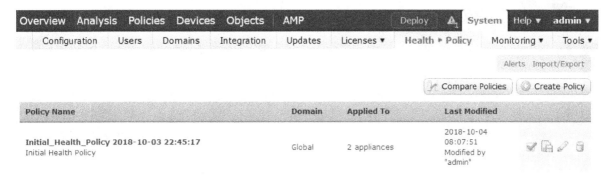

You can create custom health policies to view and monitor the device status such as interface traffic, memory and CPU utilization , SLA, High Availability, AMP status etc.

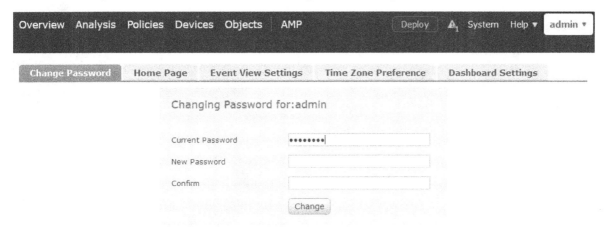

The current user settings can be viewed from the user tab. As I am logged in as admin, the tab shows the current user name. You can change the password, customize the dashboard, and change the event view settings, time zone etc from here.

Register Cisco FTD with Cisco FMC.

At this stage, we have our Cisco FTD device and Cisco FMC ready, configured with management IP address. Now we can add Cisco FTD in to Cisco FMC. We have already configured the manager in FTD with the FMC IP address and the registration key.

```
> configure manager add 192.168.45.25 123456
Manager successfully configured.
Please make note of reg_key as this will be required while adding Device in FMC
>
```

Now let's add FTD in to FMC. Navigate to **Devices -> Device management** and click on **Add,** and **Add device.**

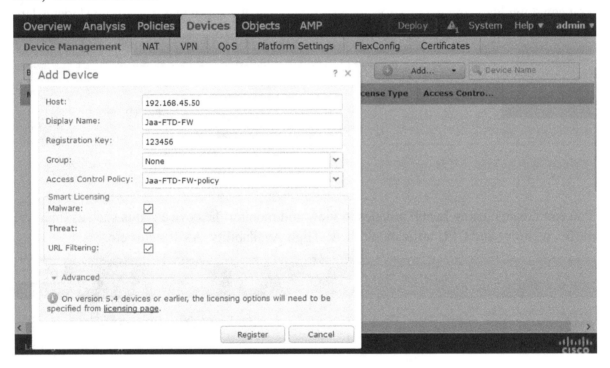

You will get a popup window to add a device.

In the Host field, enter the IP address of the Cisco FTD device. Then you can give a hostname for the device. Enter the same registration key that is configured on FTD. In this case 123456. If you want to add the device in to a group, you can add. I will explain that in the following sections.

You need to provide an Access Control Policy for the firewall. This is mandatory. You can either create the Access Control Policy before add the device itself or with doing this add, you can create a policy. Click on the dropdown menu and select **Create new policy.**

You will get another window to create a new policy. In the Name field, enter a name. Then a description. If you want to inherit the policy from any other existing policy, then you can select it in the Select base policy section.

Provide the default action for the policy. In my case, I am selecting Network Discovery. What Network discovery does is, it will discover all the interface and associated network details. The other two default actions are Block all traffic and Intrusion Prevention. You should be very careful while selecting this, because this will be the implicit rule for your FTD access list.

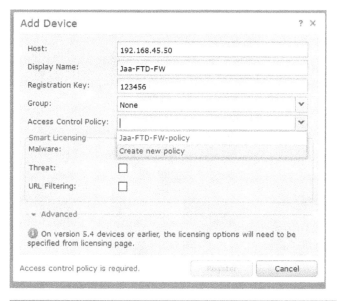

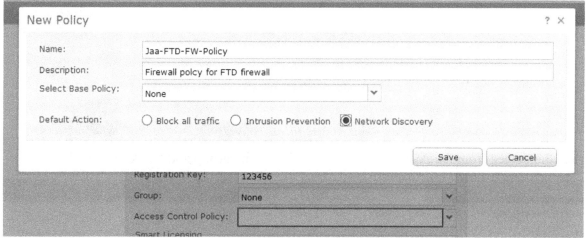

After creating the policy, select the licensing for the FTD device. I have enabled all the three available licenses. Then click on Register.

The FTD will scan and discover all the details of the FTD firewall device. Once the registration is successful, you can see the newly add device in the Devices page.

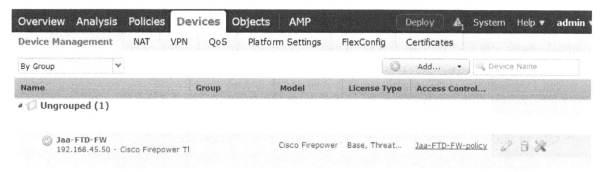

If you want to group this device, then click on Add, and Add group. For illustrating this, I have created a group for HQ-Location and added the newly added FTD in to that.

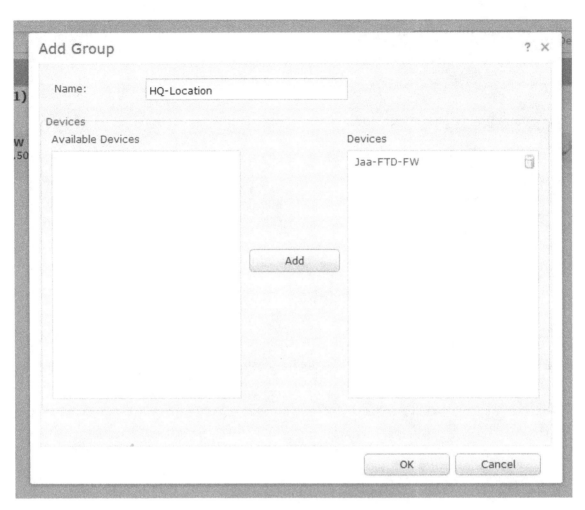

Add the device from the Available devices section to the group and Click OK to add.

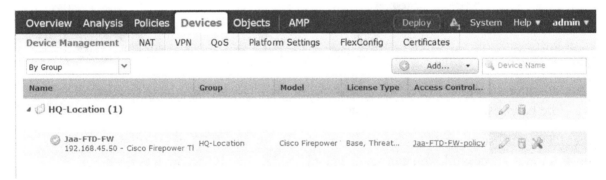

Now you can see the device user the group HQ-Location. This is useful when you have multiple firewalls in a location. Also when you apply firewall rules in to multiple firewall, this grouping will helps.

Now let's access this newly added FTD. Click on the firewall **Jaa-FTD-FW.** You can see the Firewall dashboard with many details such as health, routing, interfaces, etc. Try exploring each tabs to understand and familiarize with the graphical interface.

I will be explaining each tabs, how to configure interfaces, add routing etc. in the coming sections.

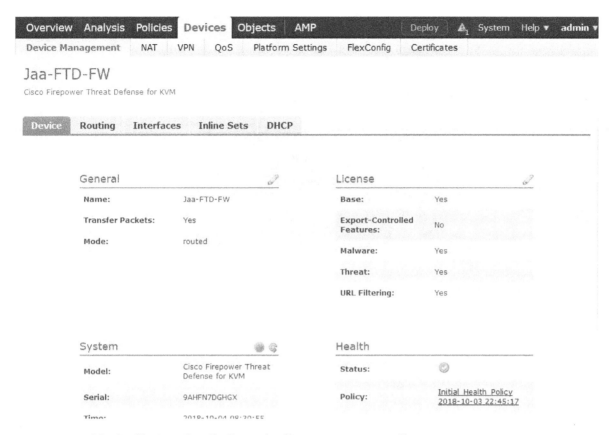

You can verify the license details from the license page as well.

Go to **System -> Licenses, Smart Licenses**

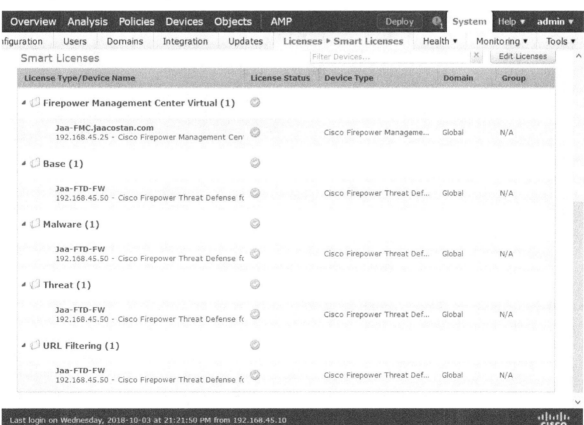

Now you can see that the device has been added to each license category. Remember, for fully using the Next Generation Firewall features, you must have the Malware, Threat and URL filtering licenses.

You can also verify the FTD-FMC integration status from the cisco FTD CLI as well using **show managers** command.

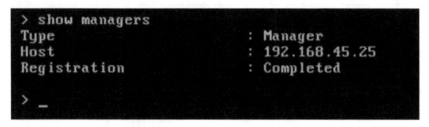

So the Integration has been successful. From here onwards, we will be using only the Cisco Firepower Management Centre for Managing the Cisco FTD devices.

Configure the Firewall Zone and Interface

Note that there is a major difference in the zone configuration on FTD. Unlike in ASA firewall, there is no interface Security Level in FTD

We can create the firewall zones in two ways. One way is to create the zone from the **Objects** tab. When we have a planned network, we might create all the zones and other network objects first before proceeding with the configurations.

The second way is you can create the zone while configuring the Network interface of the FTD device. To be familiar with both options, in this lab, I will create the inside zone from the Object tab and the outside zone from the **Device->Interfaces** tab

Ok, let's create a zone from the Object tab. The zone configuration is similar to the ASA **nameif** concept, except that there is no security level concept in Cisco FTD.

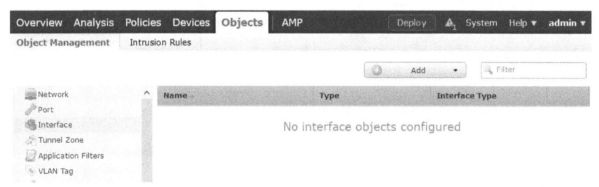

Go to the **Objects -> Object Management** tab. Click on **Interface**

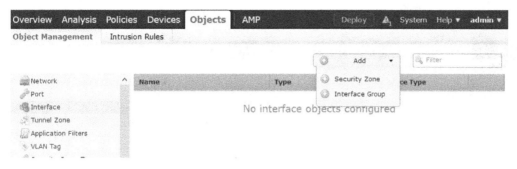

To create a Zone, click on **Add, Security Zone.**

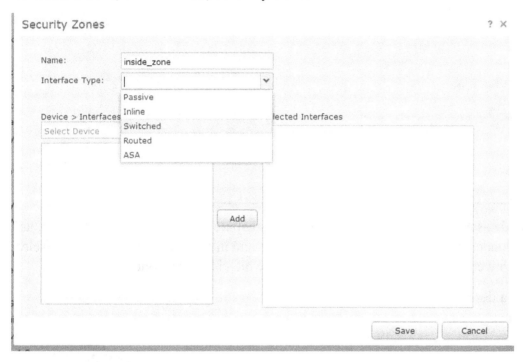

Provide a logical name for the Security zone. As per this lab topology, I am creating a zone called **inside_zone** and selecting the interface type as **Routed.** Then click on Save.

The zone has been created. Now we need to assign this zone to an interface of the FTD.

Go to the Devices -> Device Management and click on the FTD device that we have added in to the FMC.

Go to the interfaces tab and select the interface.

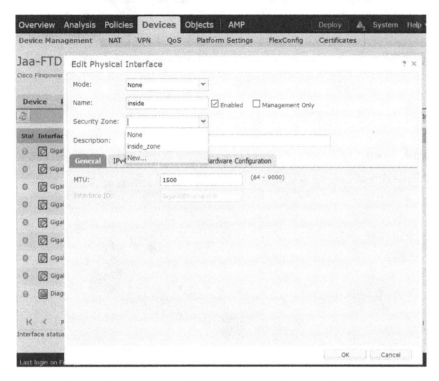

Select the mode as None (There are two other modes that are applicable for IPS devices), and give a name. I have given the interface name as inside and in the Security Zone section, select the zone which we have created in the previous step, which is inside_zone.

You can give a description for the interface.

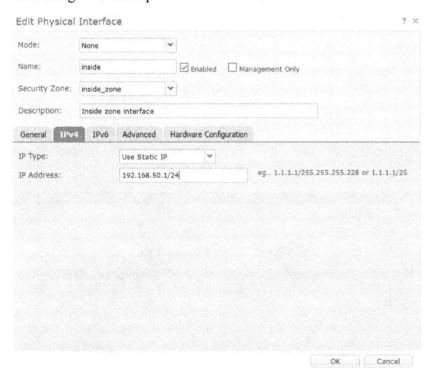

Provide the interface IP address from the IPv4 tab. 192.168.50.1/24 as per the lab topology. And click OK.

Now you need to save the configuration before deploying it. This step is similar to the configuration change in PaloAlto firewalls. Save the configurations and then Deploy it to make the changes in effect.

Once you save it and click on Deploy, it will give a confirmation window.

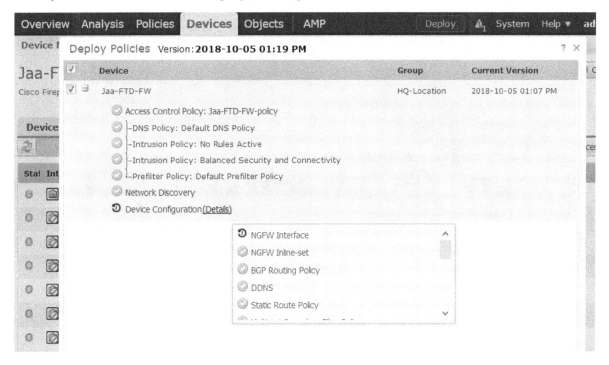

Here you need to select the device which you need to apply the configuration. I have selected the device Jaa-FTD-FW. Then deploy it.

You can see the deployment status next to deploy button.

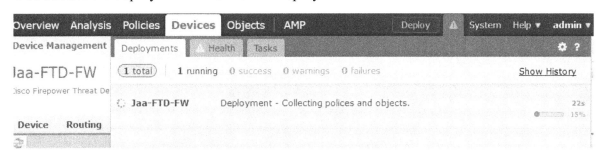

Once the deployment is successful, it will give an alert.

Now let's create the outside zone directly from the interface level.

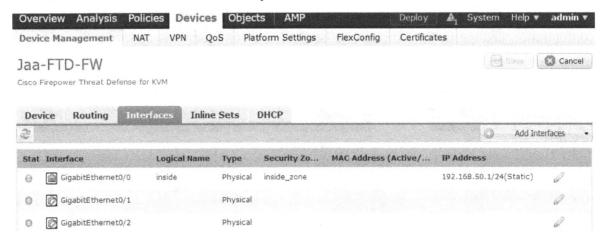

Edit the GigabitEthernet0/1 interface.

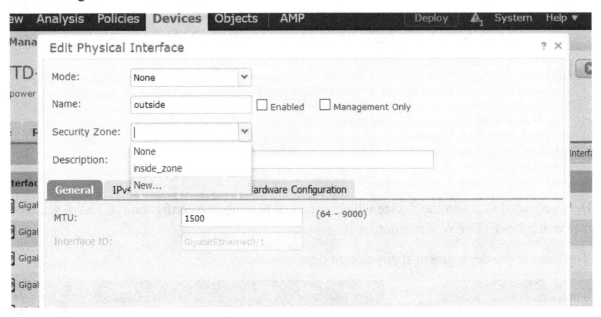

While selecting the Security zone drop down menu, click on New to create a new zone.

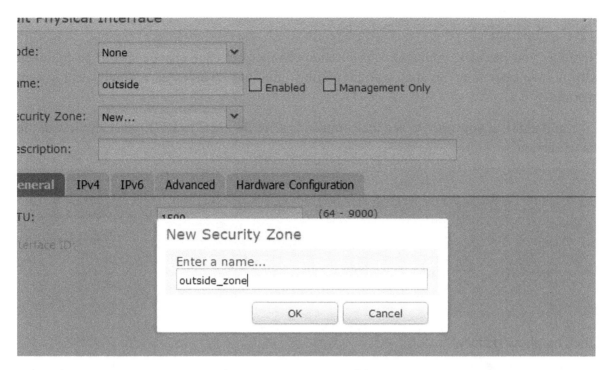

Enter the zone name. Here I put the zone name as outside_zone.

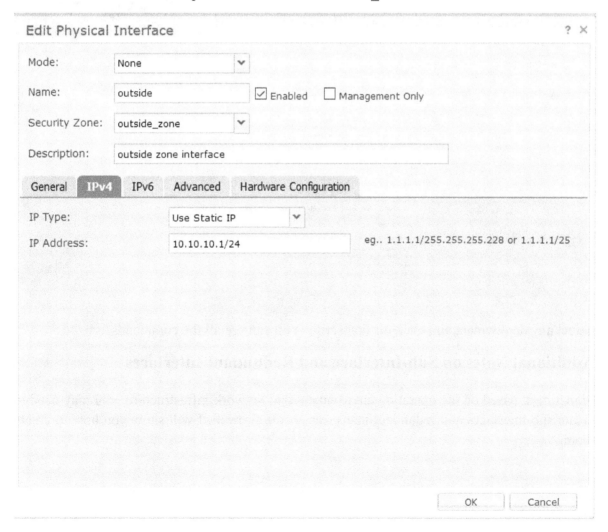

I have assigned the outside interface IP as 10.10.10.1/24. And click OK.

Follow the same procedure, save and deploy.

Note that you can make multiple configuration changes but each change should be followed with a save operation. So that you can deploy multiple changes as a single deployment operation.

Like in ASDM, if you want to see the commands send by FMC to FTD, you can view at the status section.

Click on Show History.

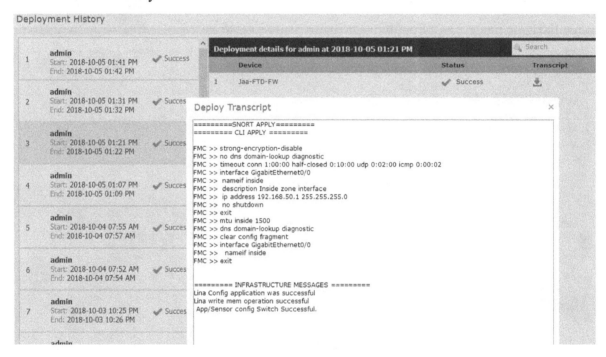

Select any deployment and click on Transcript. You can see all the commands.

Additional Notes on Sub-Interface and Redundant Interfaces

Sometimes, based on the operating environment and network infrastructure, you may need to create sub-interfaces and redundant interfaces on the firewall. I will show you how to create them.

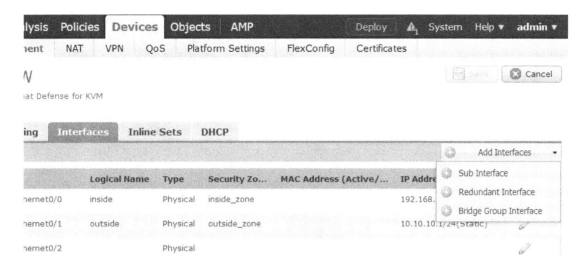

If you need to create a Sub Interface, click on Add Interface and select Sub Interface.

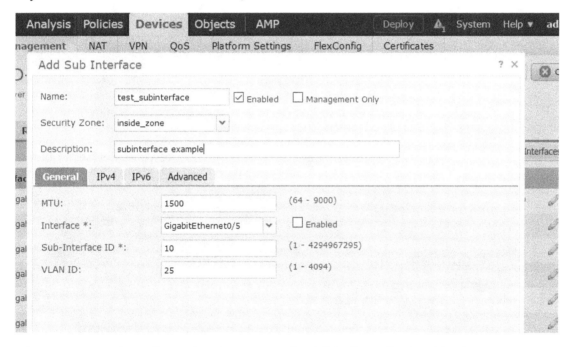

The concept and configuration is same as in ASA firewall. Provide the name, zone , sub-interface ID and the VLAN ID. Then provide the IP address and click OK.

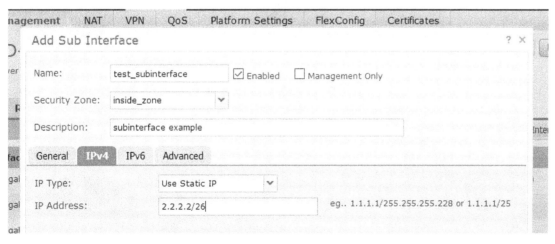

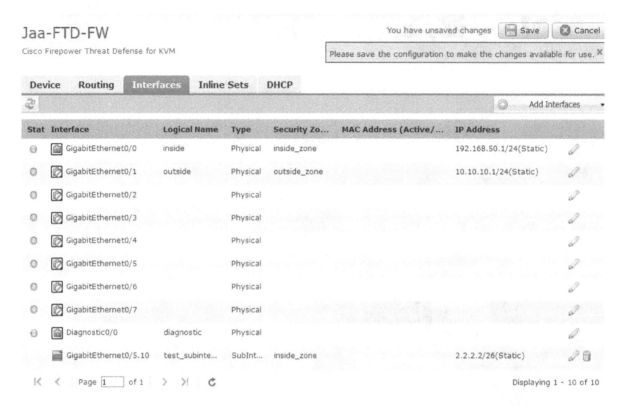

You can see the newly created sub-interface from the Interfaces tab,

Mostly, you may have multiple redundant links for some of the firewall interface. Like as shown in the diagram.

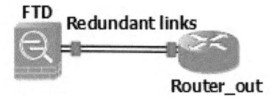

To create redundant links, Select Redundant Interface option.

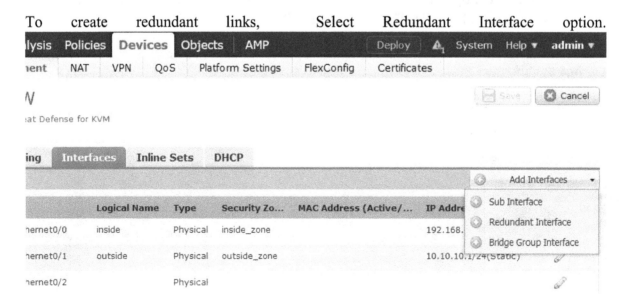

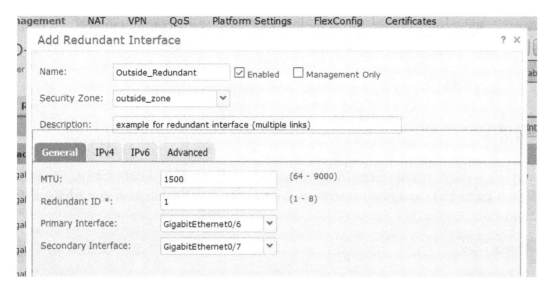

Provide a Redundant ID and select the primary and secondary interfaces. Enter the IP address from the IPv4 tab.

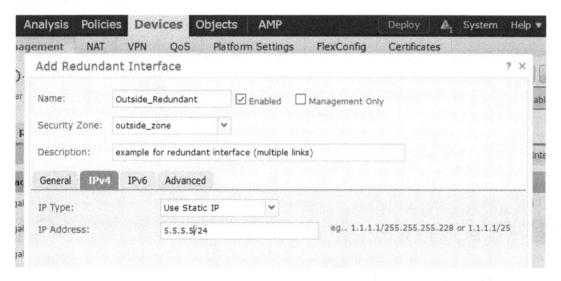

You can view the Redundant interface from the Interfaces tab.

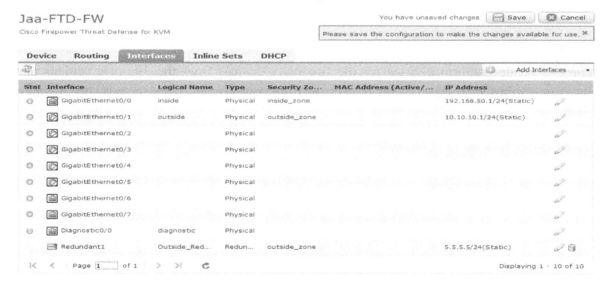

So the basic IP addressing on the firewall interface and zone configurations has been completed. If you like, you may go to the FTD CLI and verify the interface configuration.

```
>
> show interface ip brief
Interface              IP-Address      OK? Method Status               Prot
ocol
GigabitEthernet0/0     192.168.50.1    YES manual up                    up
GigabitEthernet0/1     10.10.10.1      YES manual up                    up
GigabitEthernet0/2     unassigned      YES unset  administratively down up
GigabitEthernet0/3     unassigned      YES unset  administratively down up
```

Also you can do a **show running-config** to view the configuration. Look for the security level, by default cisco FTD assign all interfaces with a zero level value as it don't have any significance on FTD.

```
.
NGFW Version 6.2.0
!
hostname firepower
enable password 8Ry2YjIyt7RRXU24 encrypted
strong-encryption-disable
names
!
!
interface GigabitEthernet0/0
 description Inside zone interface
 nameif inside
 cts manual
  propagate sgt preserve-untag
  policy static sgt disabled trusted
 security-level 0
 ip address 192.168.50.1 255.255.255.0
!
interface GigabitEthernet0/1
 description outside zone interface
 nameif outside
 cts manual
  propagate sgt preserve-untag
  policy static sgt disabled trusted
 security-level 0
 ip address 10.10.10.1 255.255.255.0
!
```

Also note that, you need to write the command completely. **show running-config** will work but **show run** won't work. This is a major change in FTD. Use the Tab key to autocomplete the commands.

Create a Platform Policy

You can create platform policies for the firepower devices from the platform settings tab. Platform settings are used to set the banner, security compliances and system related settings. There are two kinds of platform policies. Firepower Settings Policy and Threat Defense Settings Policy. Threat defense policy is specific to the FTD devices and the other one if for the firepower devices from Cisco.

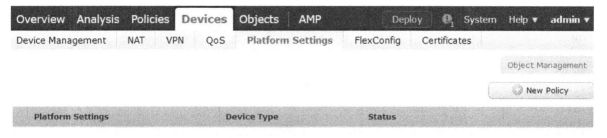

Click on New Policy and create a Threat Defense Settings.

New Policy   ? ✕

Name: FTD_platform_policy

Description: platform policy for FTD devices

Targeted Devices

Select devices to which you want to apply this policy.

Available Devices   Selected Devices

🔍 Search by name or value   📇 Jaa-FTD-FW   🗑

📁 HQ-Location

📇 Jaa-FTD-FW

[Add to Policy]

[Save]   [Cancel]

Provide a Platform policy name and description. Select the device or device group. The whole platform setting swill be applied to those selected appliances.

So for example, you don't need to create banner for each firewall, no need to configure syslog/NTP servers one by one. You just create all those settings as a Threat Defense Setting Policy and apply to all the devices in one go.

The first option in a platform policy is for ARP Inspection.

ARP inspection: To mitigate ARP spoofing incidents and conflicts. Firewall inspect the ARP packets and drop any conflicting traffics. You can enable the ARP inspection on the FTD interfaces.

In the next settings, you can create a banner for your FTD device.

Fragment Settings: How you want the firewall to handle the packet fragments. What number of or size of fragments you need to keep in memory etc.

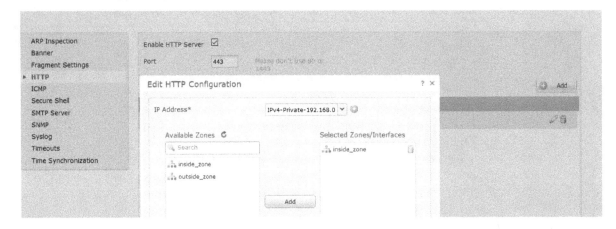

HTTP: This is to allow HTTPS access to the FRD firewall, just like we configure in ASA firewall. You can specify the allowed IP list here.

ICMP: By default ICMP works on every interface. But if you want to do some granular configuration, or block them, then you can specify it here.

Secure Shell: Allow the SSH access in to the FTD firewall. Specify the IP Addresses here.

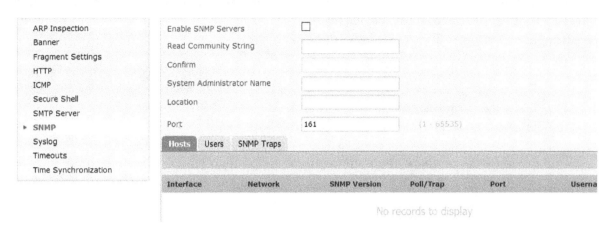

SMTP server: You can specify the SNMP server here. Additional setting such as traps and polling, you can specify under the SNMP settings.

Syslog: Specify the log servers and Email notification servers under this settings.

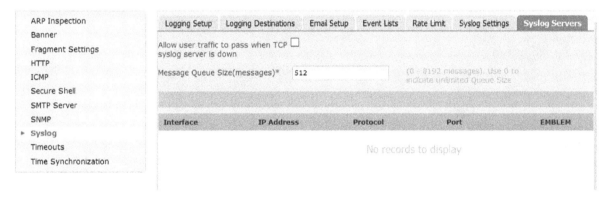

You can also configure the NTP server settings here.

After configuring the required options, Save it and Deploy to the FTD device.

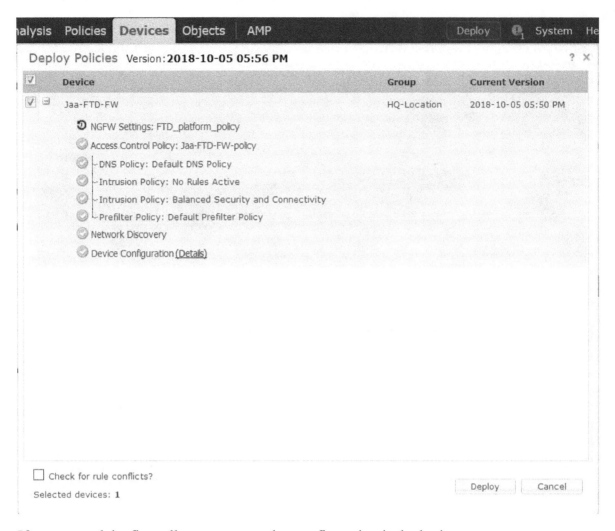

If you expand the firewall, you can see what configuration is deploying.

You can verify the settings once it is deployed. For example, the Banner.

```
AUTHORIZED USERS ONLY.

Last login: Fri Oct  5 18:48:25 2018 from 192.168.45.10

Copyright 2004-2017, Cisco and/or its affiliates. All rights reserve
Cisco is a registered trademark of Cisco Systems, Inc.
All other trademarks are property of their respective owners.

Cisco Fire Linux OS v6.2.0 (build 42)
Cisco Firepower Threat Defense for KVM v6.2.0 (build 363)

>
```

Configure Routing on Cisco FTD.

As of now and in the current version, Major routing protocols are supported except EIGRP. EIGRP was developed by Cisco itself but somehow it is missing in the FTD. I am not clear about their roadmap. May be they will add EIGRP support as well in the later version.

To configure routing, Navigate to Devices -> Device Management.

Let's create a static route for the outside device reachability.

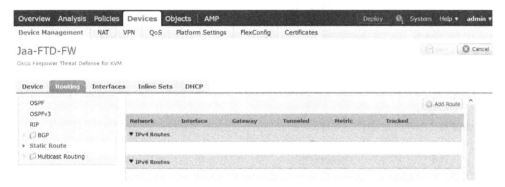

Click on Static Route and Click on Add Route.

Select the interface, the network and the gateway IP address.

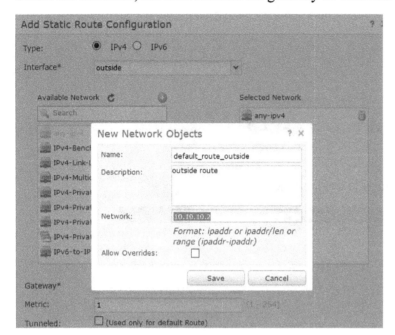

If you didn't predefine a gateway object, you can click on the green plus icon and add a new network object for the Gateway.

In my lab topology, 10.10.10.2 is the outside router IP. So I am creating a default static route here. For any traffic going to the outside, use 10.10.10.2 as the gateway.

Click OK, Save and Deploy.

Creating an OSPF route is also pretty easy using the graphical interface.

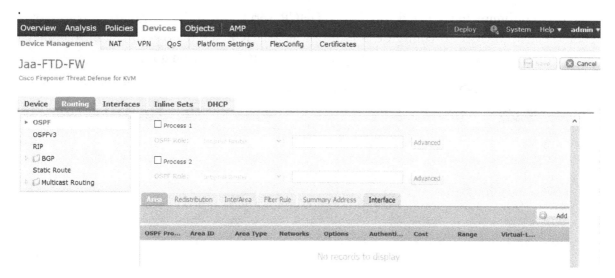

Click on OSPF, Select a Process. Here you can configure the device as an OSPF participating router, ABR/ASBR. Click on Add

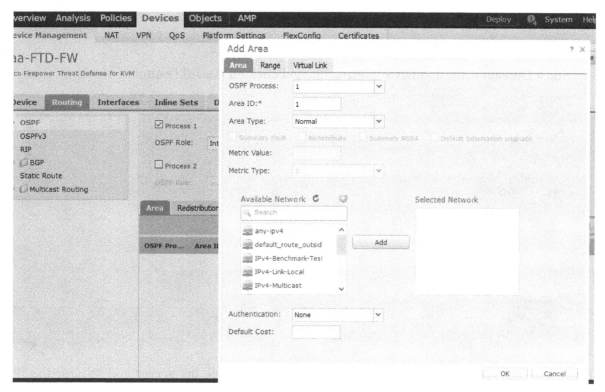

Provide the Area ID, type and select the required networks/interfaces and click OK.

If you have advanced settings, then you may configure it on the same page. As following with the existing lab topology, I am not covering the advanced routing configurations here.

Every change should be followed by a Save and deploy. Then only the changes will get in to effect.

Configuring FTD as a DHCP server

You can configure the FTD device as a DHCP server as well. Normally this is not a recommended practice to configure a Firewall as a DHCP server. But in some exceptional cases, or based on requirements, you may configure DHCP server on a Firewall.

Navigate to Devices -> Device Management -> DHCP

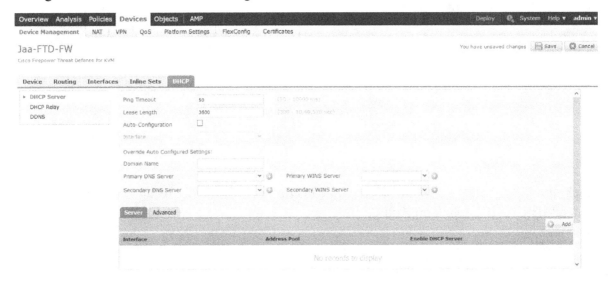

Provide a Domain name and DNS information and click on the Add button.

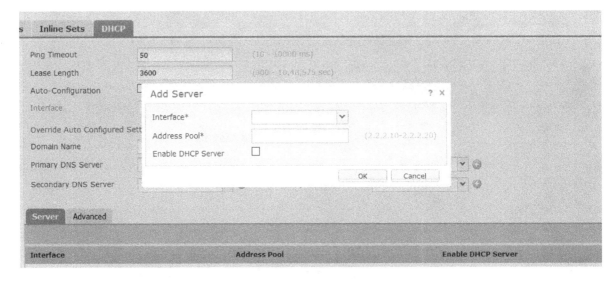

Here you need to specify which interface you need to enable the server and provide the IP address pool details. Remember to check the Enable DHCP server box and click OK.

Click on Save and Deploy.

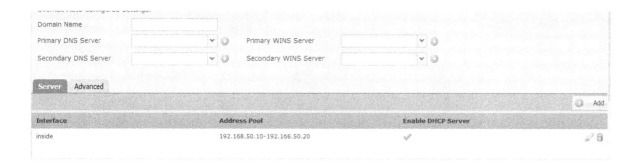

In case you need to configure DHCP Relay on FTD, then Click on DHCP Relay > Add

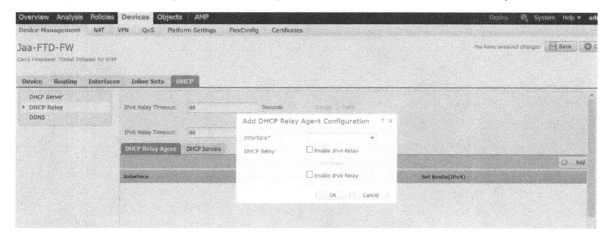

Select the Interface and click ok.

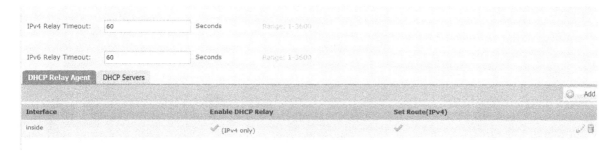

Network Address Translation (NAT)

The main function of NAT is to enable private IP Address networks to connect to the Internet. NAT replaces a private IP address with a public IP address, translating the private addresses in the internal private network into a routable addresses that can be used on the public Internet. In this way, NAT conserves public addresses and hide the network addressing of your Inside Network.

Cisco FTD NAT inherit the NAT configuration directly from the Cisco ASA. So if you are familiar with Cisco ASA, this will look similar to you.

Firepower NAT refers to the Firepower physical appliances and not the ASA with Firepower Services. For FTD, we need to select the Threat Defense NAT.We can create a NAT policy and can assign it to a device. So for different FTD firewalls, you will have multiple NAT policy respectively.

Click on Threat defense NAT.

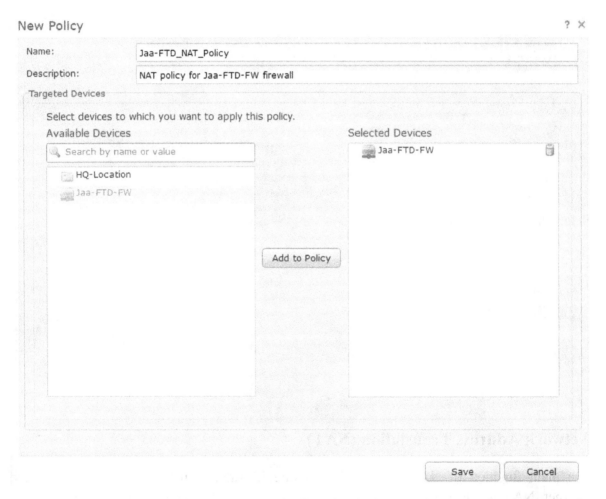

Provide a policy name and description. And select the device to which you want to apply the NAT policy. Then click on Save.

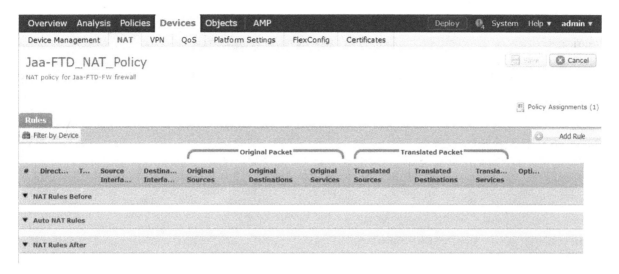

So like in ASA, there are three NAT rule sections. The order of rule checking is from top to bottom. Manual NAT lets you identify both the source and destination address in a single rule. Though Destination address translation is rarely implemented and hence it is optional.

NAT rules before and after Auto NAT are considered as Manual NAT. So in short, if we categorize NAT, there are two types. Manual NAT and Auto NAT. Auto NAT and manual NAT rules are stored in a single table that is divided into three sections. Section 1 rules are applied first, then section 2, and finally section 3, until a match is found.

1) NAT Rules before Auto NAT. All the specific Manual NAT rules will will be added in this section by default.

2) Auto NAT Rules also known as Object NAT.

3) NAT Rules after Auto NAT. If you have general NAT policy that doesn't match section 1 & 2 will go here.

Static NAT

Let's create a Static NAT rule for the inside PC. Click on Add rule.

Select the NAT rule as Manual. Since the rule is a static one, select static from the type section.

Select the source and destination interface from Interface object section. This can be considered as optional. If you don't specify an interface, it will act just like the ASA global rule.

Then go to the translation tab,

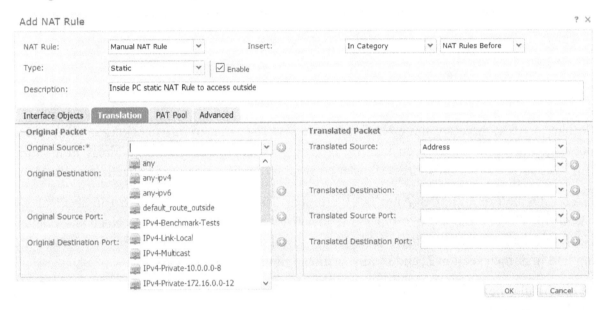

Select the source object that we need to NAT. Here in my case, it is the inside PC 192.168.50.10. If the object was not defined previously, then click on the plus icon to add the object.

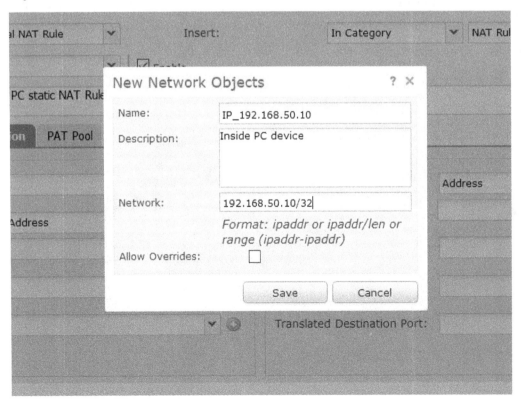

Create the object and click on save.

Now foe the translated packet section, we need to specify the mapped outside IP address. Go to translated source address. Add a new object for the mapped NAT IP. Here, I create the NAT IP as 10.10.10.5, which is in the outside network.

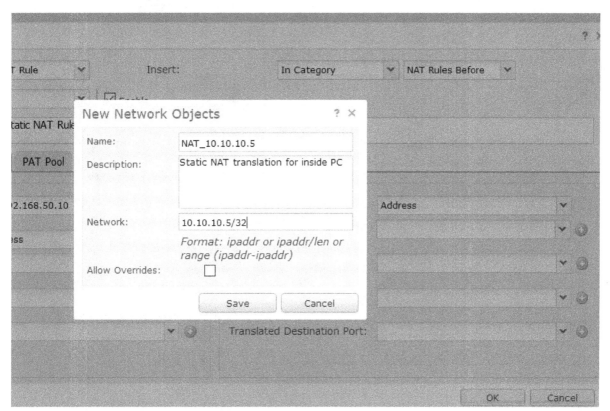

Click on Save.

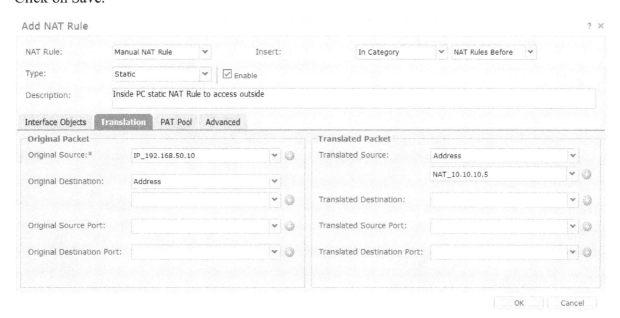

Click ok. Now you can see the NAT rule on the page.

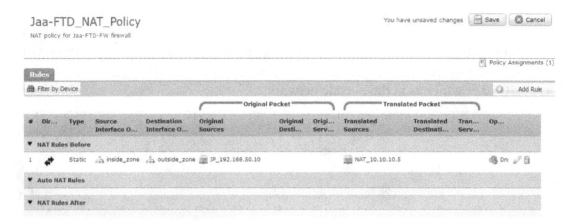

Save and deploy the NAT rule. Once it is deployed, you can verify it from the FTD device using the **show nat** command.

```
> show nat
Manual NAT Policies (Section 1)
1 (inside) to (outside) source static IP_192.168.50.10 NAT_10.10.10.5  description Inside PC static NAT Rule
to access outside
      translate_hits = 0, untranslate_hits = 0

Auto NAT Policies (Section 2)
1 (nlp_int_tap) to (inside) source static nlp_server_0_ssh_intf2 interface  service tcp ssh ssh
      translate_hits = 0, untranslate_hits = 0
> █
```

Port Address translation

Createing a PAT rule in the similar way.

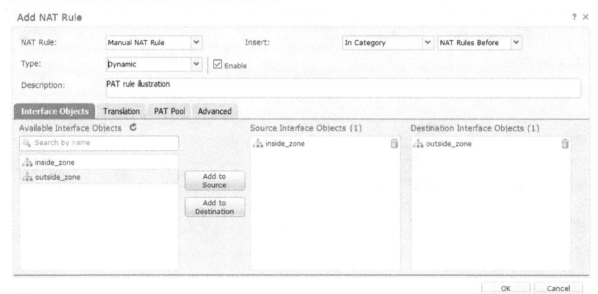

Select the source and destination zones.

Go to Translation.

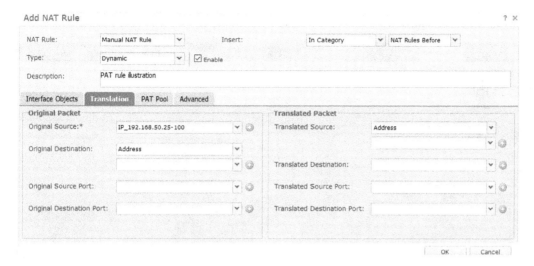

In the source, provide the IP pool. Here I created a pool 192.168.50.25-100. Then navigate to the PAT tab.

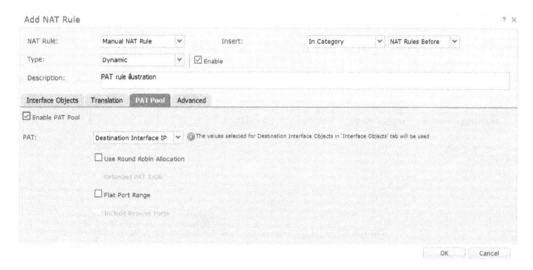

You can specify the PAT with the Interface or with a different IP or IP pool. If you select the PAT as Destination Interface IP, then it will function the traditional PAT way. All the traffic is NATed with the outside interface IP.

For illustration of PAT with multiple IP, I am creating a range of two IPs, 10.10.10.8-10.10.10.10. Click on save.

Don't confuse this with Dynamic NAT.

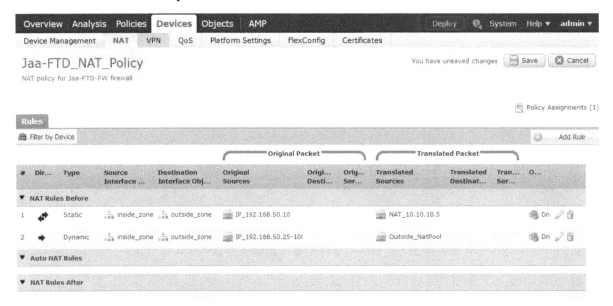

You can see that the rule has been created as a dynamic NAT rule.

In case you selected the PAT with the Destination Interface IP, you can see a similar rule like below.

Dynamic NAT

A pool of IP address can be used to NAT a range of IP address from the inside zone.

Go to Add rule,

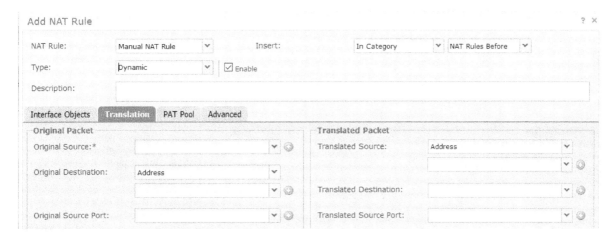

Select the type as Dynamic.

You can optionally select the source and destination interface. In the translation tab, select the source pool. I selected any IPv4 address as source. In the translation section, add a new dynamic pool for the NAT.

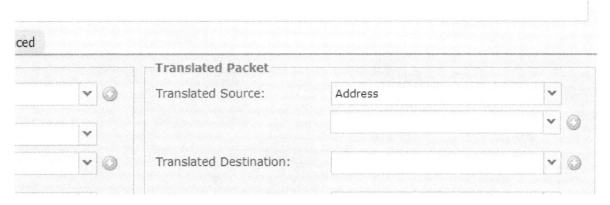

Here I created a pool 10.10.10.15-10.10.10.20.

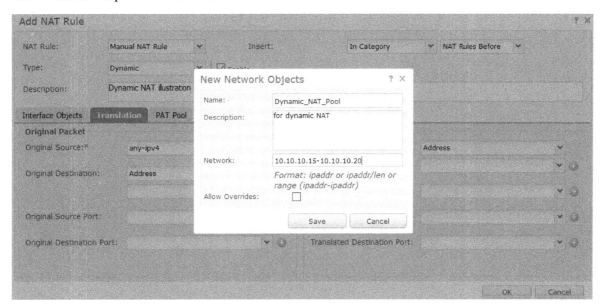

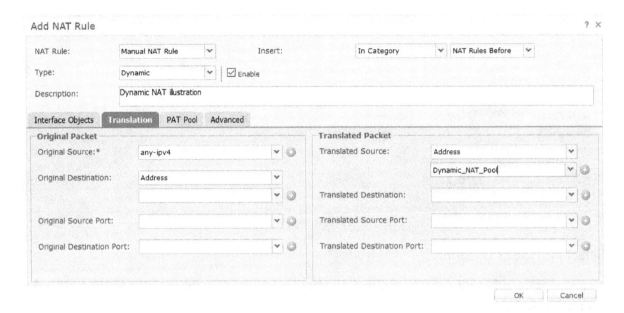

Click on OK. Now you can see the dynamic NAT rule.

Auto-NAT or Object NAT

To create an Auto-NAT rule, click on add rule, select NAT rule as Auto NAT rule.

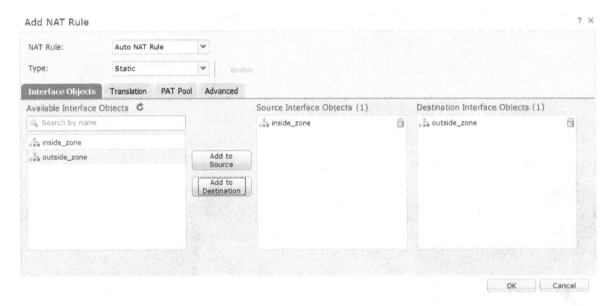

Select the source and destination interfaces/Zones.

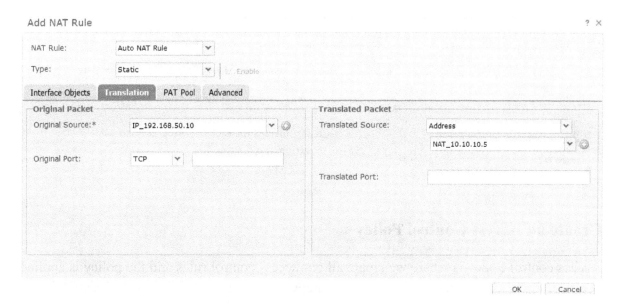

In the translation tab, select the source IP and the Translated source IP.

Here I am creating auto-NAT rule for the same insidePC 192.168.50.10 and NAT to the same 10.10.10.5 IP. Click on ok to save.

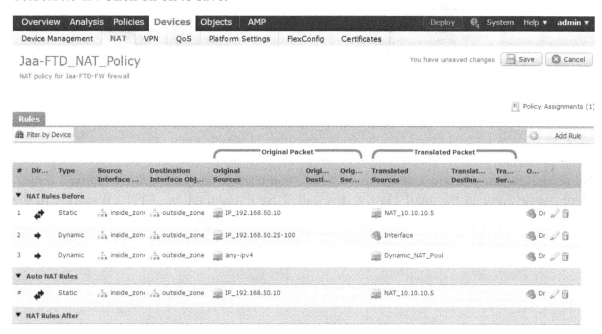

You can see the newly created NAT rule under the Auto NAT rules section. Literally, this particular rule doesn't have any significance in this case because I have already create a similar manual NAT rule above. So since NAT check sequence is first Manual NAT and then Static NAT, this newly created rule wont comes in to picture.

Finally, you can verify the rules from the FTD CLI interface as well. You can see all the rules from the CLI like in ASA firewall.

```
>
> show nat
Manual NAT Policies (Section 1)
1 (inside) to (outside) source static IP_192.168.50.10 NAT_10.10.10.5  description Inside PC static NAT Rule
to access outside
    translate_hits = 0, untranslate_hits = 0
2 (inside) to (outside) source dynamic IP_192.168.50.25-100 pat-pool interface description PAT rule illustrat
ion
    translate_hits = 0, untranslate_hits = 0
3 (inside) to (outside) source dynamic any Dynamic_NAT_Pool  description Dynamic NAT illustration
    translate_hits = 0, untranslate_hits = 0

Auto NAT Policies (Section 2)
1 (nlp_int_tap) to (inside) source static nlp_server_0_ssh_intf2 interface  service tcp ssh ssh
    translate_hits = 0, untranslate_hits = 0
2 (inside) to (outside) source static IP_192.168.50.10 NAT_10.10.10.5
    translate_hits = 0, untranslate_hits = 0
> ■
```

Create an Access Control Policy

Access control Policy is where we create all our access control rules and the policy is applied to a FTD firewall device. There is a major change on ACL in Cisco FTD with Cisco ASA. In cisco, we create the ACL rules based on the zones and interface. But with Cisco FTD, we will be creating Access control rules like a list. All the rules, whether it resides to the inside zone or outside zone or a DMZ etc. will exist together in one single Access Control Policy.

To create an Access Control Policy, Navigate to Policies tab.

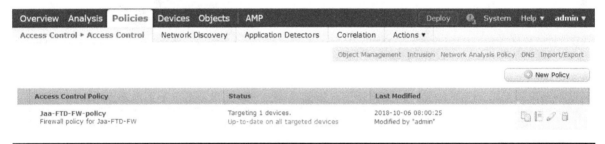

By default, when you add a device in to FMC, you need to assign a default Firewall policy. Here, while I added the Jaa-FTD-FW firewall, I have assigned Jaa-FTD-FW-policy to the FTD firewall. Hence we can see that policy in the Access control page.

Click to edit the policy.

The implicit action for this particular policy is Network Discovery only. You may change it to Deny all , allow all ,IPS actions etc.

I am setting the default action as Deny all. Means, those traffic that doesn't match the access rules will be handled by the default action.

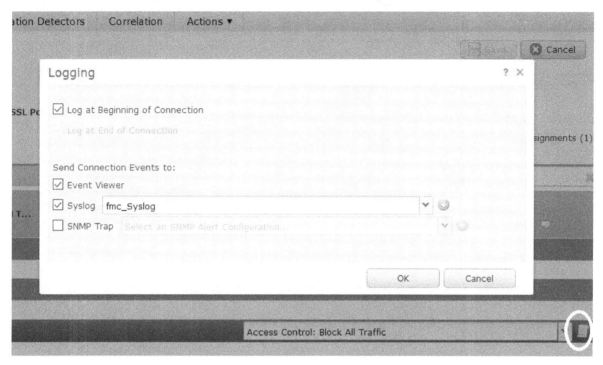

Click on the small note icon to edit the logging action. By default it is disabled and you won't be seeing any logs to the deny traffic. Enable it to set the logging on.

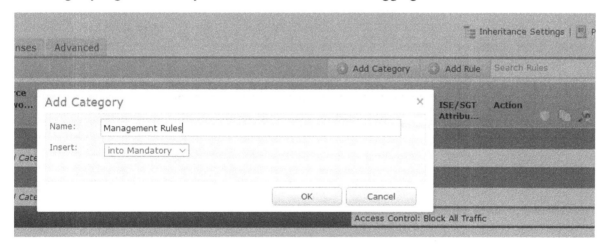

So in the Access Control policy, there are two options. One is Add category and the other one is Add rule. Add category is just like a heading or a new section. TO illustrate this, I am creating a category named as Management Rules. I can create access control rules and assign under this section.

Note that Category don't have any special functionality. It is just for creating section for arranging the rules as per your wish.

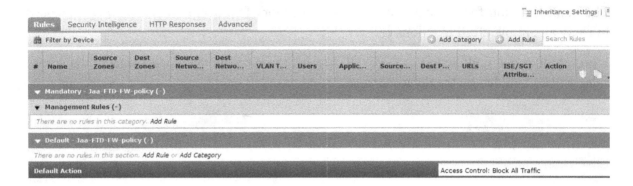

Now let's create an Access rule. Click on Add Rule.

Give a Rule name. You can also select the insert category. Since this rule I am creating is for management access of the router, I am putting this rules under the Management rules section.

Select the action as Allow. Optionally you can select the zones. In Cisco ASA, we used to create rules by specifying the zones/interfaces. But in ASA, it is optional and it acts like global rules in Cisco ASA.

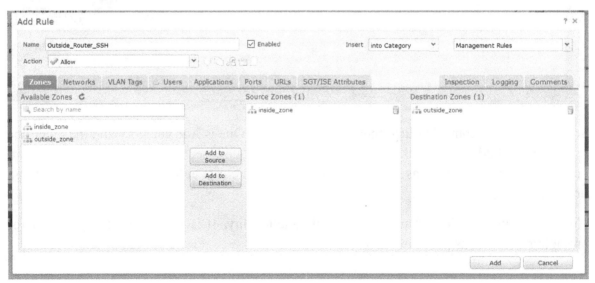

I have selected the inside zone as the source zone and the outside zone as the destination zone.

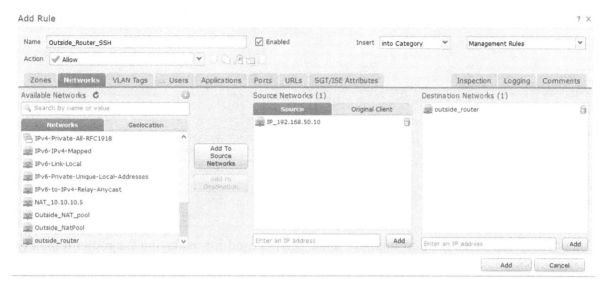

Under networks tab, select the Source object or Network. Also select the Destination networks. I have selected the source as the InsidePC and destination as the outside router.

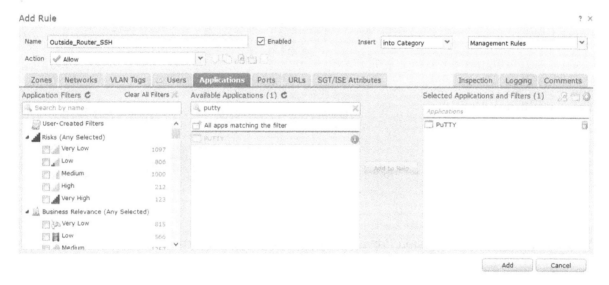

In the Application tab, we are actually make use of the NextGen features. You may select the application which you want to allow access to the destination. Here, I selected the PuTTY application for managing the destination device.

Under Ports tab, select the port number. Since SSH is used for managing the router remotely, I selected SSH.

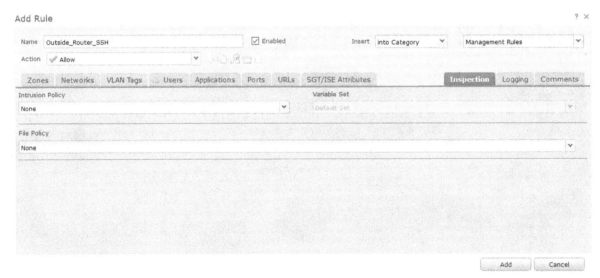

You can configure the Intrusion Prevention rules under the inspection policy.

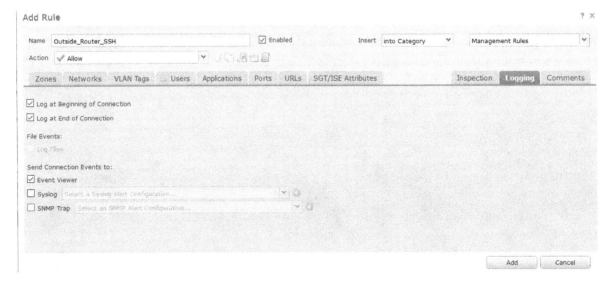

Enable logging for this particular rule. You can do this from the Logging tab.

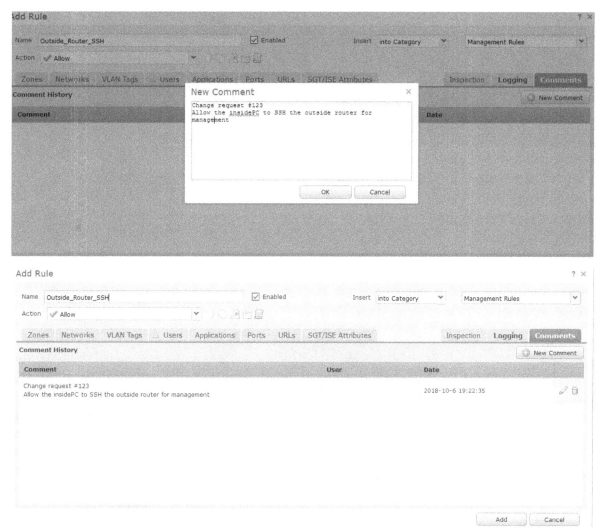

Optionally you can provide comments under the comments tab. Click OK and save the policy. Finally deploy it.

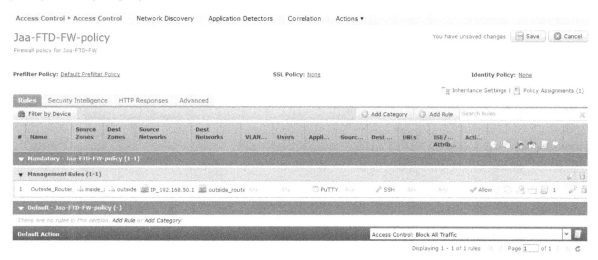

You can see the newly created rule from the Rules page. Note that the rule is placed under the Management Rules section.

Now let's create an access rule for allowing the Inside users to access the Partner website. I have already created an object for Partner website.

Provide a rule name. I have given the name as Partner_website and placed under the Mandatory section. Selected the zones as well.

Source as any (Any devices in the inside zone) and destination as the Partnet_website.

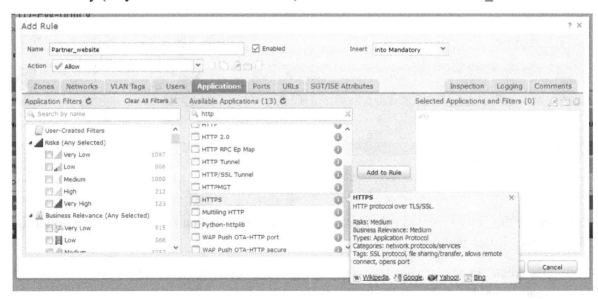

Under application setting, you can select the specific application associated with the access. Since the users are accessing the partner website, I am allowing HTTP and HTTPS application.

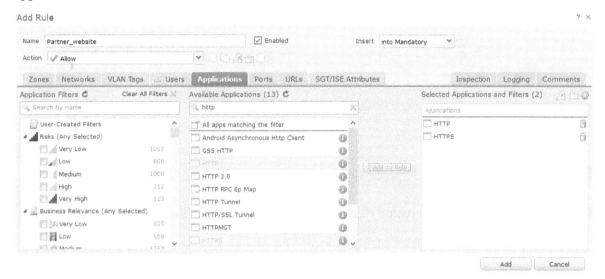

For the ports tab, select the port TCP443 and TCP80 (HTTPS and HTTP)

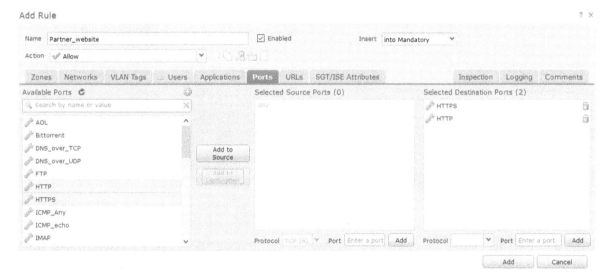

Optionally enable logging and provide a comment.

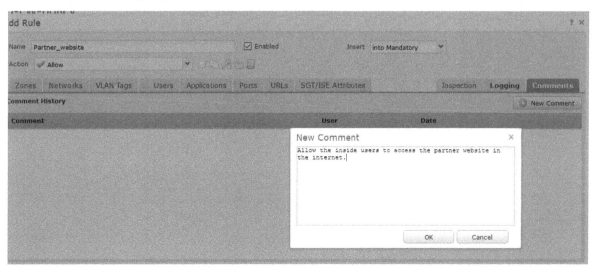

Click OK and apply the rule.

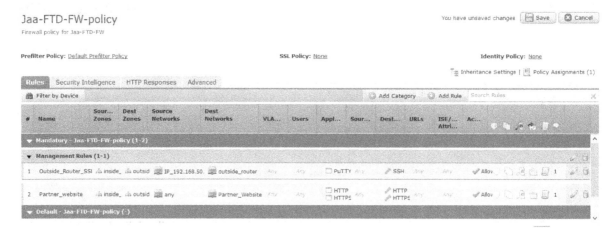

You can now see the newly created rule under the Mandatory section.

Now let's create a rule to block Facebook access for all users in the network.

Note that for this rule, I have selected the rules under management rules section. I will show you how to move a rule from one section to another.

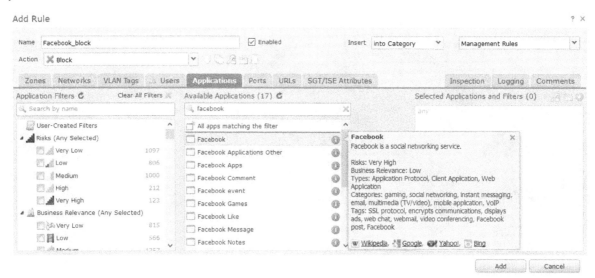

From the Application tab, select the Facebook application. Cisco also allows granular control for the applications. For example, if you want your users to access Facebook but block messaging and games, you can configure that here.

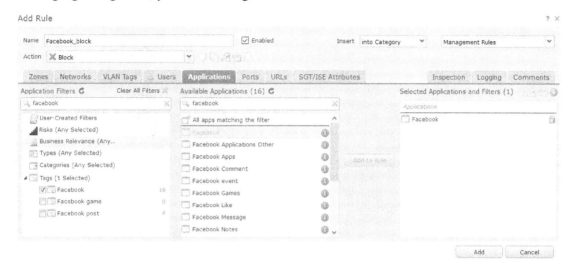

Optionally, you can block the Facebook from the URL option as well. You can specify the URL here. But for this example, I have selected the Entire Social Network URLs. This category was predefined in Cisco FTD. So if I apply, in practical it will block all the social networking websites.

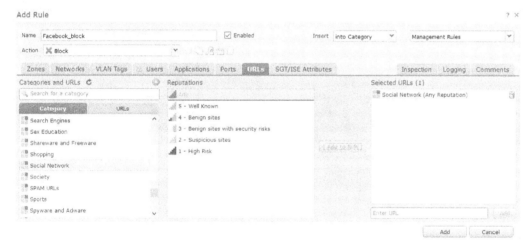

You can see that the newly created rule is placed under the Management Rules section.

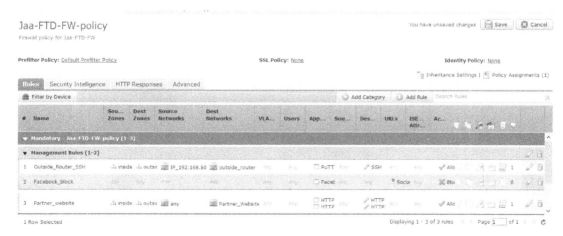

Now let's learn how to move the rule from one section to another.

Edit the rule.

You can see the move option and from the dropdown menu, select your section. I selected the section Mandatory. Click on save.

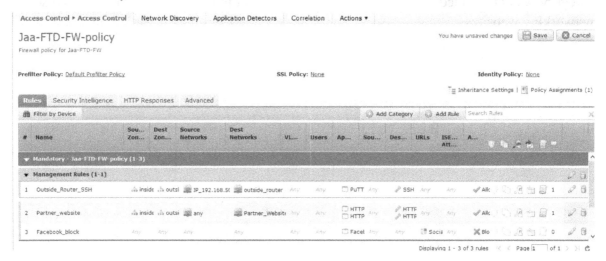

Now notice the rule has been moved out from the Management Rules section to the Mandatory section.

Always save and deploy the rules. While deploying you can see what section has the changes associated with.

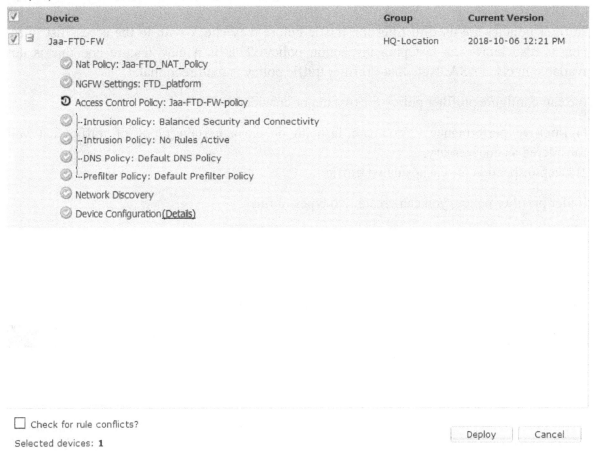

Additionally, you can view the access list from the FTD CLI also, using the same Cisco command show access-list

```
> show access-list
access-list cached ACL log flows: total 0, denied 0 (deny-flow-max 4096)
            alert-interval 300
access-list CSM_FW_ACL_; 10 elements; name hash: 0x4a69e3f3
access-list CSM_FW_ACL_ line 1 remark rule-id 9998: PREFILTER POLICY: Default Tunnel and Priority Policy
access-list CSM_FW_ACL_ line 2 remark rule-id 9998: RULE: DEFAULT TUNNEL ACTION RULE
access-list CSM_FW_ACL_ line 3 advanced permit ipinip any any rule-id 9998 (hitcnt=0) 0xf5b597d6
access-list CSM_FW_ACL_ line 4 advanced permit 41 any any rule-id 9998 (hitcnt=0) 0x06095aba
access-list CSM_FW_ACL_ line 5 advanced permit gre any any rule-id 9998 (hitcnt=0) 0x52c7a066
access-list CSM_FW_ACL_ line 6 advanced permit udp any eq 3544 any range 1025 65535 rule-id 9998 (hitcnt=0) 0x46d7839e
access-list CSM_FW_ACL_ line 7 advanced permit udp any range 1025 65535 any eq 3544 rule-id 9998 (hitcnt=0) 0xaf1d5aa5
access-list CSM_FW_ACL_ line 8 remark rule-id 268436484: ACCESS POLICY: Jaa-FTD-FW-policy - Mandatory/1
access-list CSM_FW_ACL_ line 9 remark rule-id 268436484: L7 RULE: Outside_Router_SSH
access-list CSM_FW_ACL_ line 10 advanced permit tcp ifc inside object IP_192.168.50.10 ifc outside object outside_router object-group SSH rule-id 268436484 (hitcr
f7636f
    access-list CSM_FW_ACL_ line 10 advanced permit tcp ifc inside host 192.168.50.10 ifc outside host 10.10.10.2 eq ssh rule-id 268436484 (hitcnt=0) 0x65106323
access-list CSM_FW_ACL_ line 11 remark rule-id 268436485: ACCESS POLICY: Jaa-FTD-FW-policy - Mandatory/2
access-list CSM_FW_ACL_ line 12 remark rule-id 268436485: L7 RULE: Partner_website
access-list CSM_FW_ACL_ line 13 advanced permit tcp ifc inside any ifc outside object Partner_website object-group HTTPS rule-id 268436485 (hitcnt=0) 0xee132902
access-list CSM_FW_ACL_ line 13 advanced permit tcp ifc inside any ifc outside host 120.130.140.150 eq https rule-id 268436485 (hitcnt=0) 0x619997e6
    access-list CSM_FW_ACL_ line 14 advanced permit tcp ifc inside any ifc outside object Partner_website object-group HTTP rule-id 268436485 (hitcnt=0) 0x529a58b0
    access-list CSM_FW_ACL_ line 14 advanced permit tcp ifc inside any ifc outside host 120.130.140.150 eq www rule-id 268436485 (hitcnt=0) 0x6f5f8b4d
access-list CSM_FW_ACL_ line 15 remark rule-id 268436486: ACCESS POLICY: Jaa-FTD-FW-policy - Mandatory/3
access-list CSM_FW_ACL_ line 16 remark rule-id 268436486: L7 RULE: Facebook_block
access-list CSM_FW_ACL_ line 17 advanced permit ip any any rule-id 268436486 (hitcnt=0) 0xa1d3780e
access-list CSM_FW_ACL_ line 18 remark rule-id 268434432: ACCESS POLICY: Jaa-FTD-FW-policy - Default/1
access-list CSM_FW_ACL_ line 19 remark rule-id 268434432: L4 RULE: DEFAULT ACTION RULE
access-list CSM_FW_ACL_ line 20 advanced deny ip any any rule-id 268434432 event-log flow-start (hitcnt=0) 0x97aa021a
> 
```

Pre-Filter Policy

Prefilter policies are used to filter the traffic before they check with to the access list rules. This is also known as fast path inspection policy. This is a new feature and this is not available in cisco ASA. Note that Prefilter traffic policy is unidirectional.

We can configure prefilter policy for two major considerations.

1) Improve performance - You can fastpath or block certain types of traffic that you considered as unnecessary.
2) Deep inspection for encapsulated traffic

Under prefilter policy, you can create two types of rules.

1) Tunnel rules.
2) Prefilter rules.

To create a prefilter policy, navigate to Policies -> Access Control -> Prefilter.

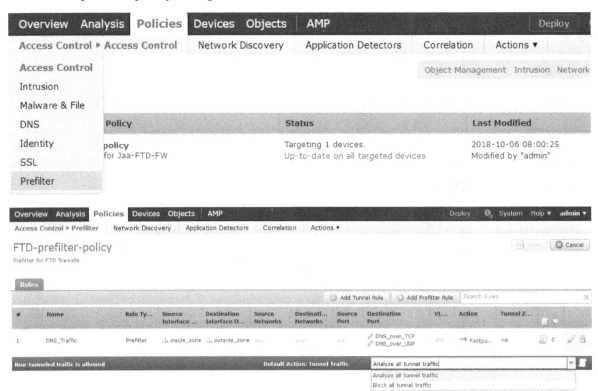

By default, there is a Default prefilter policy which will analyses all the tunnel traffic.

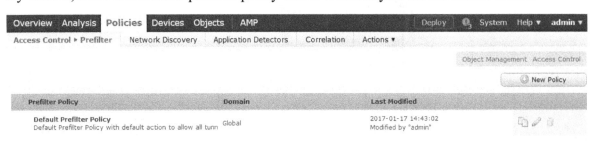

Click on New Policy.

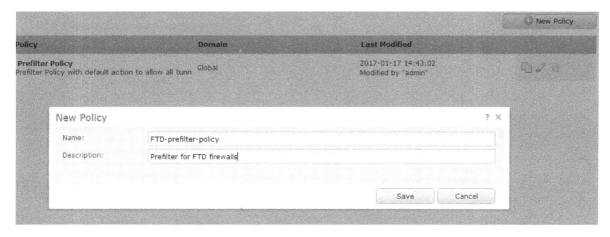

Let's create new policy. Here I am creating a policy for my FTD device named FTD-prefilter-policy.

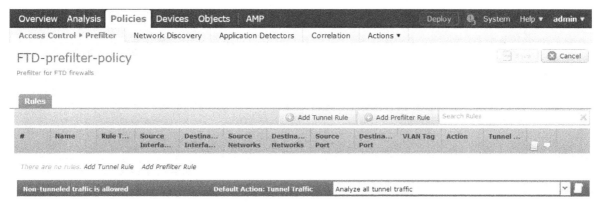

The policy has been created. Now we need to add rules in to the policy.

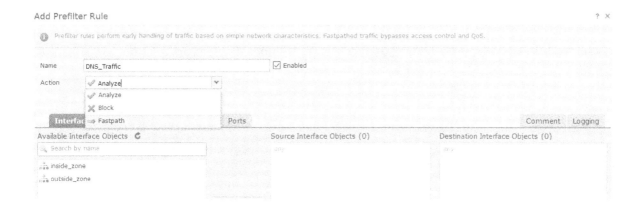

When you create a policy, you can see that there are three action that you can select.

1. Analyze means the traffic will be passed to the inspection engine for further analysis.
2. Block means block this kind of traffic.
3. Fastpath means you are trusting this traffic and no further analysis is required.

This rules is for DNS traffic. I trust my DNS traffic and I don't want deep inspection. So I selected fastpath as the action.

Also select the source and destination zone.

If you want to specify any host or network, specify it under the network section.

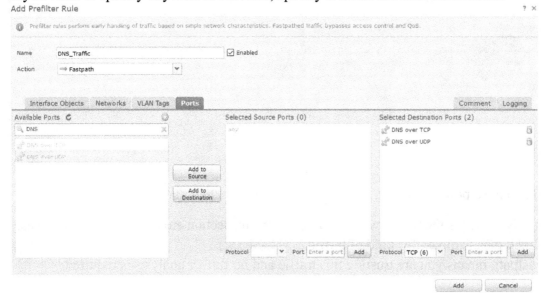

User Ports tab, I selected DNS over TCP and DNS over UDP as my destination ports. Optionally allow loggings and give comments.

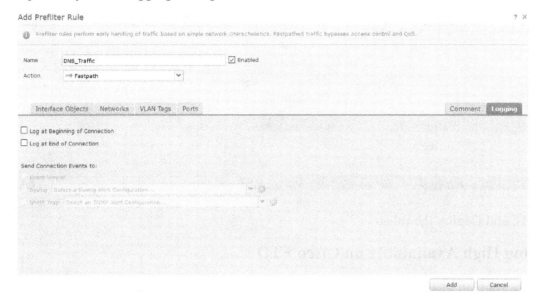

Click Add.

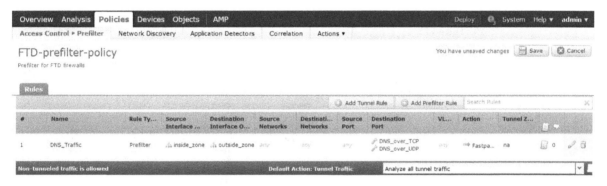

You can see the prefilter policy rule from the rules page.

Now let's create another prefilter policy to block any SSH traffic coming from outside.

Select the action as block and select the destination ports SSH. I have selected the interfaces source as outside and destination as Inside.

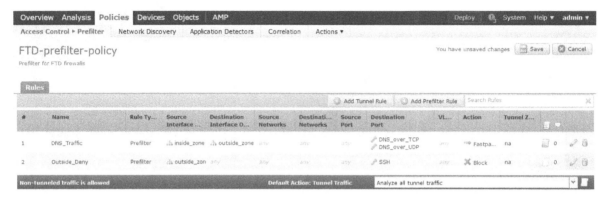

Click on Save and Deploy the rules.

Configuring High Availability on Cisco FTD

We can configure high availability on FTD devices through FMC in a pretty easy way.

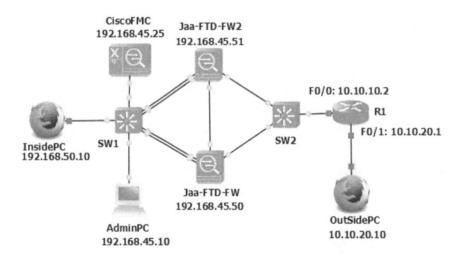

I configure a new firewall and joined it with the FMC device.

```
System initialization in progress. Please stand by.
You must change the password for 'admin' to continue.
Enter new password:
Confirm new password:
You must configure the network to continue.
You must configure at least one of IPv4 or IPv6.
Do you want to configure IPv4? (y/n) [y]:
Do you want to configure IPv6? (y/n) [n]:
Configure IPv4 via DHCP or manually? (dhcp/manual) [manual]:
Enter an IPv4 address for the management interface [192.168.45.45]: 192.168.45.5
1
Enter an IPv4 netmask for the management interface [255.255.255.0]:
Enter the IPv4 default gateway for the management interface [192.168.45.1]:
Enter a fully qualified hostname for this system [firepower]: Jaa-FTD-FW2
Enter a comma-separated list of DNS servers or 'none' []: none
Enter a comma-separated list of search domains or 'none' []: none
If your networking information has changed, you will need to reconnect.
For HTTP Proxy configuration, run 'configure network http-proxy'

Configure firewall mode? (routed/transparent) [routed]:
Configuring firewall mode ...
```

I have assigned the management IP as 192.168.45.51/24. You don't need to configure anything else on FTD device except the physical connectivity.

Once assigned the Management IP, add the new FTD device in FMC.

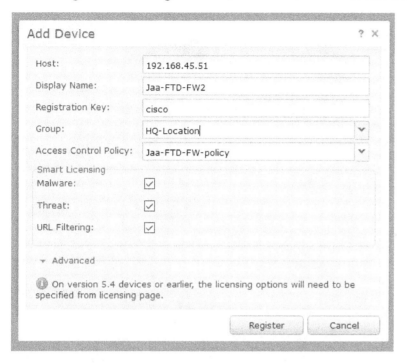

I have assigned the same policy as in the other firewall.

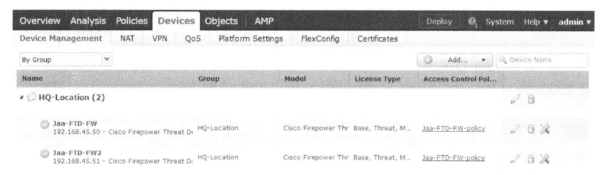

Register the device and FMC will try to discover the FTD. Once the process is finished, you can see the new FTD in the device section.

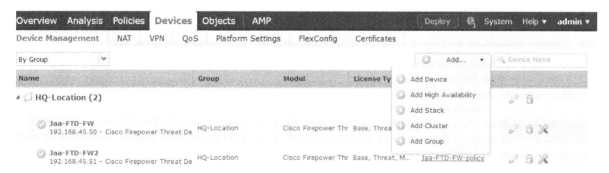

Now to configure a High Availability pair, click on Add and select Add High Availability.

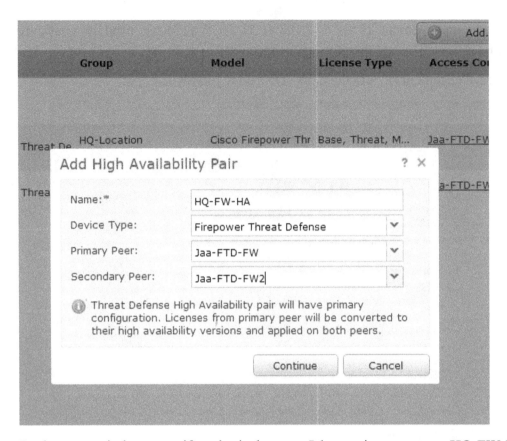

In the new window, specify a logical name. I have given a name HQ-FW-HA. Select the device type as Firepower Threat Defense. Select the primary and secondary peer. As per the topology, the primary firewall is Jaa-FTD-FW and the secondary is Jaa-FTD-FW2. Click on Continue.

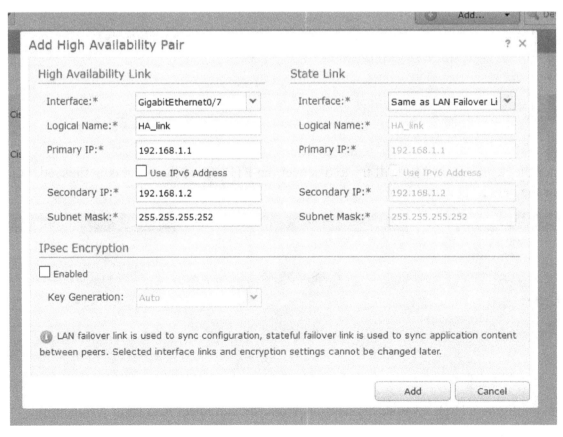

In this page, you need to specify the High Availability link and State link details. The concept is same like in Cisco ASA. As per topology, I am using a single link for both High Availability and State link.

I configured GigabitEthernet0/7 on both devices as my HA link. Provide a primary and secondary IP for the link. If you have a separate link, then you can configure the state link with another interface. Here, since it's using the same link, I selected **Same as LAN Failover Link** in the State Link interface dropdown menu. Click on Add.

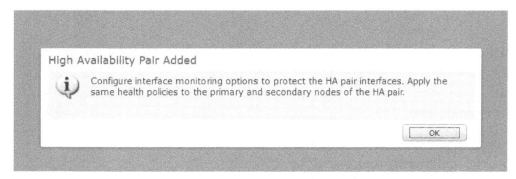

FMC will give a confirmation.

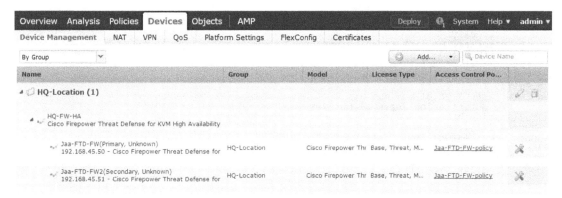

Now you can see a new HQ-FW-HA entity has been created on the devices section and the devices are shown under that. FMC will do a thorough discovery and deployment of health policies. This process may take some time.

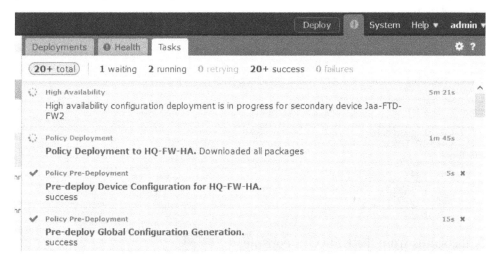

You can view the status from the Notifications section.

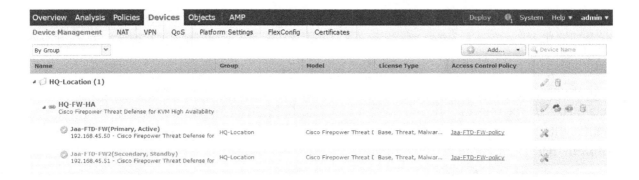

Once the configuration is finished, you can see the devices as ready.

```
> show running-config failover
failover
failover lan unit secondary
failover lan interface HA_link GigabitEthernet0/7
failover replication http
failover link HA_link GigabitEthernet0/7
failover interface ip HA_link 192.168.1.1 255.255.255.252 standby 192.168.1.2
>
>
>
> show failover
Failover On
Failover unit Secondary
Failover LAN Interface: HA_link GigabitEthernet0/7 (up)
Reconnect timeout 0:00:00
Unit Poll frequency 1 seconds, holdtime 15 seconds
Interface Poll frequency 5 seconds, holdtime 25 seconds
Interface Policy 1
Monitored Interfaces 3 of 61 maximum
MAC Address Move Notification Interval not set
failover replication http
version: Ours 9.7(1)4, Mate 9.7(1)4
Serial Number: Ours 9A1QN245J81, Mate 9AL5HR5NQ4X
Last Failover at: 02:20:56 UTC Oct 7 2018
        This host: Secondary - Standby Ready
                Active time: 0 (sec)
```

```
> show running-config failover
failover
failover lan unit primary
failover lan interface HA_link GigabitEthernet0/7
failover replication http
failover link HA_link GigabitEthernet0/7
failover interface ip HA_link 192.168.1.1 255.255.255.252 standby 192.168.1.2
>
>
> show failover
Failover On
Failover unit Primary
Failover LAN Interface: HA_link GigabitEthernet0/7 (up)
Reconnect timeout 0:00:00
Unit Poll frequency 1 seconds, holdtime 15 seconds
Interface Poll frequency 5 seconds, holdtime 25 seconds
Interface Policy 1
Monitored Interfaces 3 of 61 maximum
MAC Address Move Notification Interval not set
failover replication http
version: Ours 9.7(1)4, Mate 9.7(1)4
Serial Number: Ours 9AL5HR5NQ4X, Mate 9A1QN245J81
Last Failover at: 02:51:21 UTC Oct 7 2018
        This host: Primary - Active
                Active time: 389 (sec)
                slot 0: empty
```

Also you can verify the status from the FTD CLI console.

Use show running-config failover command and show failover commands to see the status.

Now proceed with the HA configurations.

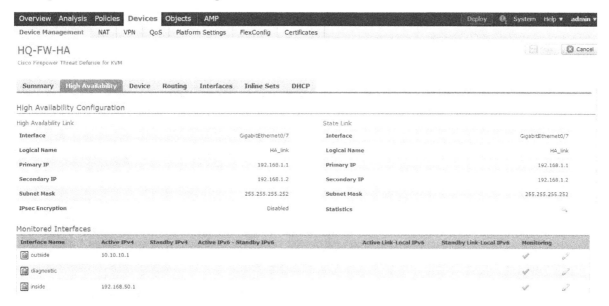

Get in to the HQ-FW-HA (the newly created failover group) from the device management page. You can see a new tab named as High Availability in the page.

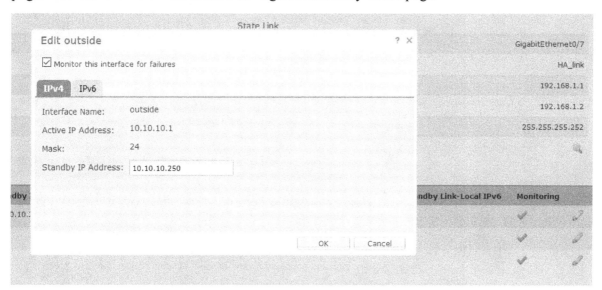

Now we need to add the standby IP addresses for the firewall interfaces.

Click on outside, and edit. I have provided the standby IP as 10.10.10.250. IF you want to enable monitoring, just check the Monitor Interface checkbox.

Similarly add standby IP for the inside interface as well.

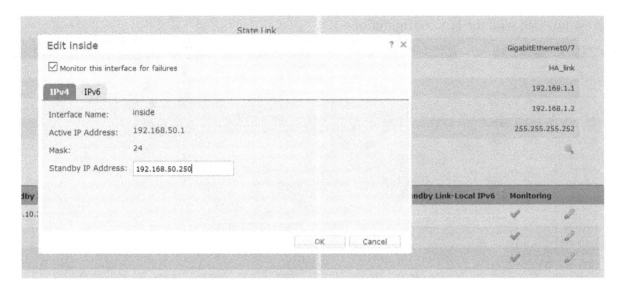

The standby IP for the inside interface is 192.168.50.250.

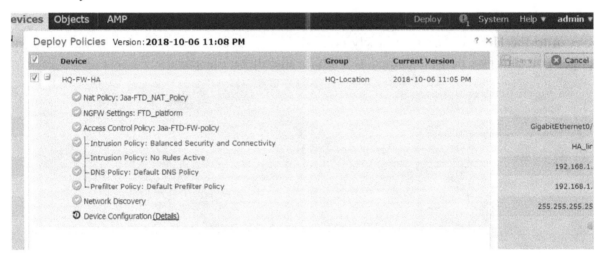

Save and deploy the change. Also Note that, while deploying, we are now not deploying to individual FTD devices. We are deploying to the HA pair.

Verify the configuration from FTD CLI.

```
CiscoFMC    192.168.45.50  ×    192.168.45.51

> show running-config interface gi0/0
!
interface GigabitEthernet0/0
 description inside interface
 nameif inside
 cts manual
  propagate sgt preserve-untag
  policy static sgt disabled trusted
 security-level 0
 ip address 192.168.50.1 255.255.255.0 standby 192.168.50.250
> show running-config interface gi0/1
!
interface GigabitEthernet0/1
 description outside interface
 nameif outside
 cts manual
  propagate sgt preserve-untag
  policy static sgt disabled trusted
 security-level 0
 ip address 10.10.10.1 255.255.255.0 standby 10.10.10.250
>
```

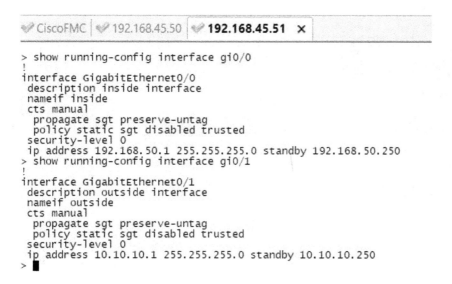

```
> show running-config interface gi0/0
!
interface GigabitEthernet0/0
 description inside interface
 nameif inside
 cts manual
  propagate sgt preserve-untag
  policy static sgt disabled trusted
 security-level 0
 ip address 192.168.50.1 255.255.255.0 standby 192.168.50.250
> show running-config interface gi0/1
!
interface GigabitEthernet0/1
 description outside interface
 nameif outside
 cts manual
  propagate sgt preserve-untag
  policy static sgt disabled trusted
 security-level 0
 ip address 10.10.10.1 255.255.255.0 standby 10.10.10.250
> █
```

Optionally, if you want to provide a static ARP entry for the HA pair, you can give at the Interface Mac Addresses section. This helps the device to stick a same mac address during the failover.

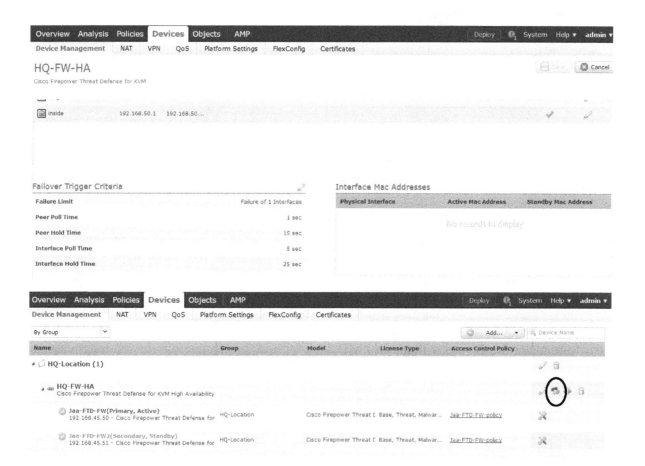

If you want to force a failover, you can click on the small icon under the HA pair.

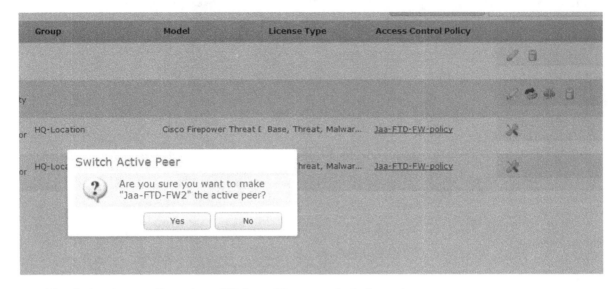

It will ask for the confirmation. Click on Yes to switch the pair.

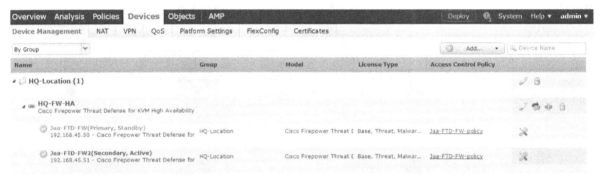

You can see the change. The primary become standby and the secondary become primary.

Summary

So in the last few chapters, we discussed and learned how to configure cisco FTD and Cisco FMC, how to integrate them and do all the configurations such as Interface settings, ACLs, NAT, routing, High Availability, and how to manage the firewall from FMC. I hope it gave you a broad overview on the FTD firewall configurations and confident that you can configure a FTD firewall or an FMC devices easily and efficiently.

In the next section, we are going to see how to upgrade a Cisco ASA firewall to FTD and how to manage the device without an FMC.That is; how to manage the device locally using Firepower Device Manager.

Upgrading Cisco ASA firewall to FTD.

Installing Cisco FTD image on an existing ASA Firewall.

Before proceeding, do take a complete backup of your existing ASA firewall including license keys and software before proceeding with the next steps which will erase the configuration and all files. Also as a pre-requisite ensure the Cisco ASA appliance is running rommon version v1.1.8 or greater by using an IOS command show module to ensure re-imaging will be successful. If the rommon version is older than v1.1.8 then the ASA Appliance needs a rommon upgrade.

Reboot ASA and break the startup/boot sequence
During the boot process hit Break or Esc to interrupt boot:

```
Use BREAK or ESC to interrupt boot.
Use SPACE to begin boot immediately.
Boot in 10 seconds.

Boot interrupted.
Management0/0
Link is DOWN
MAC Address: ############
Use ? for help.
rommon #1>
```

Now upload the Boot Image and Boot the ASA Firewall

We now need to configure the necessary parameters on the ASA Firewall to download the Cisco Firepower Threat Defense Boot Image. Ensure you have an FTP/TFTP server installed and configured to allow the Firewall to download the image files.
Next, configure the ASA Firewall with the necessary network settings/variables so it can access the image and system files previously downloaded. ASA 5555-X firewall uses a built-in management interface, hence no need to specify the management interface.

```
rommon #1> address 192.168.45.45
rommon #2> server 192.168.45.3
rommon #3> gateway 192.168.45.1
rommon #4> file ftd-boot-9.7.1.0.cdisk
rommon #5> set
ROMMON Variable Settings:
```

```
ADDRESS=192.168.45.45
SERVER=192.168.45.3
GATEWAY=192.168.45.3
PORT=Management0/0
VLAN=untagged
IMAGE=ftd-boot-9.7.1.0.cdisk
CONFIG=
LINKTIMEOUT=20
PKTTIMEOUT=4
RETRY=20
```

Rommon Variables explained:-
- Address: IP address of Cisco Firewall
- Server: The TFTP server from where the firewall will download the image
- Gateway: The IP address of the network gateway.
- File: The name of the boot image file
- Set: Shows the rommon settings

The Sync command will save the NVRAM parameters, and updates the configuration changes.
```
rommon #6> sync
```
Updating NVRAM Parameters...

```
rommon #7> ping 192.168.45.3
Sending 20, 100-byte ICMP Echoes to 192.168.45.3, timeout is 4
seconds:
!!!!!!!!!!!!!!!!!!!!!
Success rate is 100 percent (20/20)
```

So the TFTP server is reachable from the firewall.

```
rommon #7> tftpdnld
ROMMON Variable Settings:
ADDRESS=192.168.45.45
SERVER=192.168.45.3
GATEWAY=192.168.45.3
PORT=Management0/0
VLAN=untagged
IMAGE=ftd-boot-9.7.1.0.cdisk
CONFIG=
LINKTIMEOUT=20
PKTTIMEOUT=4
RETRY=20

tftp ftd-boot-9.7.1.0.cdisk@192.168.45.3
!!!!!!!!!!!!!!!!!!!!!!!!!!!!!!!!!!!!!!!!!!!!!!!!!!!!!!!!!!!!!!!!!!!!!!
!!!!!!!!!!
```

```
Received 107292672 bytes

Launching TFTP Image...

Execute image at 0x14000

Cisco Security Appliance admin loader (3.0)
Platform ASA5XXX

Loading...
IO memory blocks requested from bigphys 32bit: 125055
INIT: version 2.88 booting

Starting udev
Configuring network interfaces... done.
Populating dev cache
Found device serial number F#########.
Found USB flash drive /dev/sdc
Found hard drive(s): /dev/sda /dev/sdb
fsck from util-linux 2.23.2
dosfsck 2.11, 12 Mar 2005, FAT32, LFN
There are differences between boot sector and its backup.
Differences: (offset:original/backup)
65:01/00
Not automatically fixing this.
/dev/sdc1: 62 files, 825465/2011744 clusters
Launching boot CLI ...
Configuring network interface using DHCP
Bringing up network interface.
Depending on your network, this might take a couple of minutes
when using DHCP...
ifup: interface lo already configured
Using IPv6 address: fe80::2f6:63ff:feda:e623
IPv4 address not assigned. Run 'setup' before installation.
INIT: SwitchingStarting system message bus: dbus.
Starting OpenBSD Secure Shell server: sshd
generating ssh RSA key...
generating ssh ECDSA key...
generating ssh DSA key...
Could not load host key: /etc/ssh/ssh_host_ed25519_key
done.
Starting Advanced Configuration and Power Interface daemon:
acpid.
acpid: starting up
acpid: 1 rule loaded
acpid: waiting for events: event logging is off
```

```
Starting ntpd: done
Starting crond: OK


      Cisco FTD Boot 6.0.0 (9.7.1.)
Type ? for list of commands
CiscoFTD-boot>
```

Check TFTP/FTP server connectivity by pinging the server.

```
CiscoFTD-boot> ping 192.168.45.3
PING 192.168.45.3 (192.168.45.3) 56(84) bytes of data.
64 bytes from 192.168.45.3: icmp_seq=1 ttl=128 time=0.722 ms
64 bytes from 192.168.45.3: icmp_seq=2 ttl=128 time=0.648 ms
64 bytes from 192.168.45.3: icmp_seq=2 ttl=128 time=0.856 ms
--- 192.168.45.3 ping statistics ---
3 packets transmitted, 3 received, 0% packet loss, time 2018ms
rtt min/avg/max/mdev = 0.648/0.742/0.856/0.086 ms
```

Now the boot image has been successfully installed and can proceed with upgrading ASA with FTD image.

Install Firepower Threat Defense System Software

Now proceed with the set up. Execute **setup** command to initiate the setup process. The setup process will gather important configuration parameters for the FTD device such as Hostname, IP address, Subnet mask, Gateway, DNS servers etc.

```
CiscoFTD-boot> setup

                       Welcome to Cisco FTD Setup
                       [hit Ctrl-C to abort]
                       Default values are inside []

Enter a hostname [CiscoFTD]: CiscoFTD
Do you want to configure IPv4 address on management
interface?(y/n) [Y]: y
Do you want to enable DHCP for IPv4 address assignment on
management interface?(y/n) [Y]: n
Enter an IPv4 address: 192.168.45.45
Enter the netmask: 255.255.255.0
Enter the gateway: 192.168.45.1
Do you want to configure static IPv6 address on management
interface?(y/n) [N]: n
Stateless autoconfiguration will be enabled for IPv6 addresses
Enter the primary DNS server IP address: 192.168.45.3
Do you want to configure Secondary DNS Server? (y/n) [n]: n
Do you want to configure Local Domain Name? (y/n) [n]: y
```

```
Enter the local domain name: jaacostan.com
Do you want to configure Search domains? (y/n) [n]: n
Do you want to enable the NTP service? [Y]: n
Please review the final configuration:

Hostname:                         CiscoFTD
Management Interface Configuration

IPv4 Configuration:               static
        IP Address:               192.168.45.45
        Netmask:                  255.255.255.0
        Gateway:                  192.168.45.1

IPv6  Configuration:                              Stateless
autoconfiguration
DNS Configuration:
        Domain:                   jaacostan.com
        DNS Server:               192.168.45.3

NTP configuration:                Disable

CAUTION:
You have selected IPv6 stateless autoconfiguration, which
assigns a global address based on network prefix and a device
identifier. Although this address is unlikely to change, if it
does change, the system will stop functioning correctly.
We suggest you use static addressing instead.

Apply the changes?(y,n) [Y]: Y
Configuration saved successfully!
Applying...
Restarting network services...
Done.
Press ENTER to continue...
```

At this point the appliance's initial configuration phase is complete and ready to begin downloading the FTD system image

To initiate the image download use the system install ftp://192.168.45.3/ftd-6.2.0-362.pkg and replace the IP address portion with your FTP server's IP address.

During the installation, the install process will ask for the necessary credentials to authenticate to the FTP server. When the system image installation is complete, the system will require the user to hit enter to reboot.

```
CiscoFTD-boot> system install ftp://192.168.45.3/ftd-6.2.0-
362.pkg
```

```
####################### WARNING #########################
# The content of disk0: will be erased during installation! #
########################################################

Do you want to continue? [y/N]: y
Erasing disk0 ...
Extracting ...
Verifying. …

Enter credentials to authenticate with ftp server
Username: cisco
Password: Cisco12345#
Verifying. ... ...
Downloading. ... ...
Extracting. ... ...

Package Detail
          Description:                Cisco ASA-FTD 6.2.0-
362 System Install
          Requires reboot:           Yes

Do you want to continue with upgrade? [y]: y
Warning: Please do not interrupt the process or turn off the
system.
Doing so might leave system in unusable state.

Starting upgrade process.... ….. ….
Populating new system image. ….. ….

Reboot is required to complete the upgrade. Press 'Enter' to
reboot the system.

Broadcast message from root@CiscoFTD (ttyS0) (Thu Sep 16
15:04:08 2018):
The system is going down for reboot NOW!
```

The ASA FTD Appliance will now reboot. When the system has successfully booted up it
will require you to login using the default username (admin) & password (Admin123) then
require you to press Enter to present Cisco's EULA which must be accepted at the end by
pressing again the enter key or typing YES:

```
Cisco ASA5555-X Threat Defense v6.2.0 (build 362)
firepower login: admin
Password: Admin123
You must accept the EULA to continue.
Press <ENTER> to display the EULA:
```

```
END USER LICENSE AGREEMENT
IMPORTANT:  PLEASE  READ  THIS  END  USER  LICENSE  AGREEMENT
CAREFULLY.
................................. . .
Product  warranty  terms  and  other  information  applicable  to
Cisco products are
available        at        the        following        URL:
http://www.cisco.com/go/warranty.

Please enter 'YES' or press <ENTER> to AGREE to the EULA: YES
```

Finally the last step involves changing the default admin password and configuring again the system's network settings.

Similar to the previous steps, pressing enter will accept the default value shown between the brackets [ ]:

```
System initialization in progress. Please stand by.
You must change the password for 'admin' to continue.
Enter new password: Cisco123#
Confirm new password: Cisco123#
You must configure the network to continue.
You must configure at least one of IPv4 or IPv6.
Do you want to configure IPv4? (y/n) [y]: y
Do you want to configure IPv6? (y/n) [n]: n
Configure IPv4 via DHCP or manually? (dhcp/manual) [manual]:
manual
Enter  an  IPv4  address  for  the  management  interface
[192.168.45.45]: [enter]
Enter  an  IPv4  netmask  for  the  management  interface
[255.255.255.0]: [enter]
Enter the IPv4 default gateway for the management interface
[data-interfaces]: [enter]
Enter a fully qualified hostname for this system [firepower]:
jaacostan.com
Enter  a  comma-separated  list  of  DNS  servers  or  'none' []:
[enter]
Enter  a  comma-separated  list  of  search  domains  or  'none'
[]:[enter]
If your networking information has changed, you will need to
reconnect.

Manage the device locally? (yes/no) [yes]: yes
>
```

The ">" symbol indicates that the FTD setup is complete and running.

More information on the Cisco Firepower Threat Defense, can be found at Cisco website: http://www.cisco.com/c/en/us/support/security/firepower-ngfw/products-installation-guides-list.html

Manage Cisco FTD firewall using Firepower Device Manager (FDM).

Cisco Firepower Device Manager (FDM) is intended for managing the Small to Medium range of Cisco FTD devices, and when you don't have any Cisco FMC devices in your network.

You can now log into the Cisco Firepower Device Manager by entering the ASA Firewall appliance IP address in your web browser:

Once logged in, you can follow the step-by-step setup Device Setup Wizard that will take you the necessary steps to initially configure your new ASA FTD device:

Cisco Firepower Threat Defense (FTD) is the Next-Generation Firewall solution that will eventually replace the existing ASA software. Note that, it is important to understand the current limitations of FTD before upgrading the existing ASA firewall in the production environment.

Though standalone FTD firewalls can be managed using the Firepower Device Manager, it is recommended to use the feature rich Firepower Management Centre to manage all the FTD firewalls in your Network Infrastructure.

Understand the major differences of FTD with ASA.
- Unlike in traditional ASA firewall, there is no interface security level in FTD, though in CLI you can see the security level configured as zero and it really don't have any effect.
- Smart license: firepower threat license required for FTD device.
- Inside to outside rule is by default and it is allowed.
- By default NAT is enabled with outside interface PAT.
- When you use cli, you should write the command fully. You make use of the Tab key for auto completion of commands.
  eg: In traditional ASA firewall, to see the running configuration, you may execute the command **show run** or **sh run**. This method won't work with FTD. You should write the command fully as **show running-config**.

Let's get familiarize with the standalone firewall management using FTD device manager (FDM).

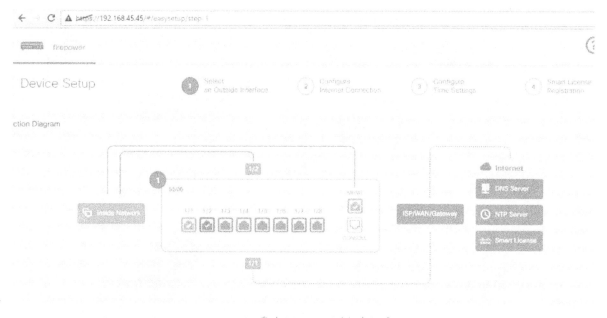

Select an outside interface

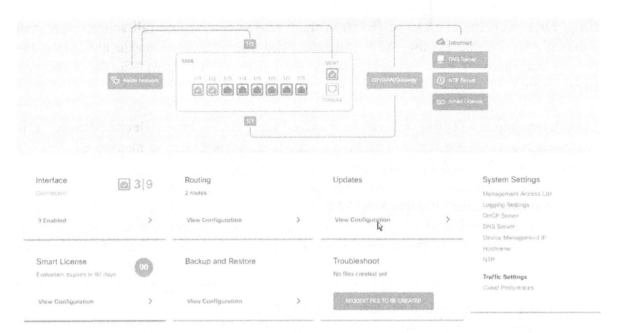

You can configure the interface settings from the Interface tab.

In this case, I am using three interfaces, inside, outside and the management. You can assign IP details.

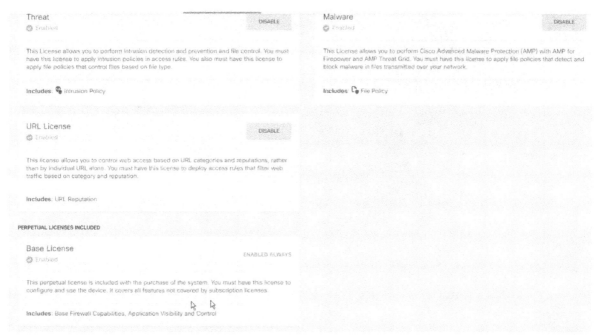

To enable license, navigate to smart licenses page. You can see the four types of licenses. Base, threat, malware and URL licenses. You can apply it here.

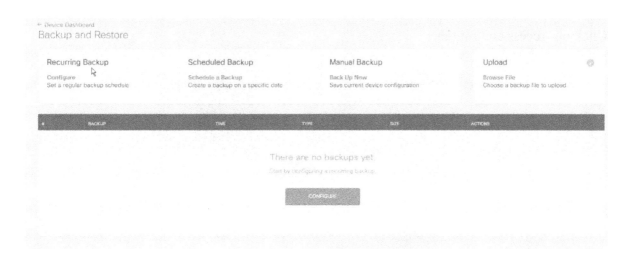

Backup the firewall configurations from the Backup and Restore page. You can schedule a backup.

To create an Access list security policy Navigate to policies tab,

Interface		Routing
Connected	3	9	2 routes
3 Enabled	>	View Configur

Click on Access control tab.

Here you can specify the access control rules.

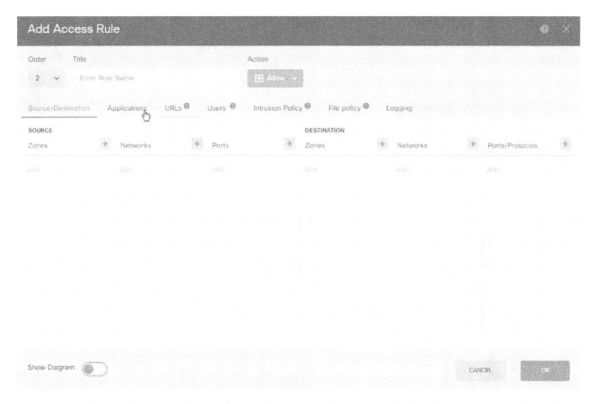

While creating rules, you have the options to selet the traditional ASA firewall options as well as the Next Generation firewall features such as URL/Application filtering, file inspection, User control and intrusion prevention rules.

You can specify the application you want to allow or block.

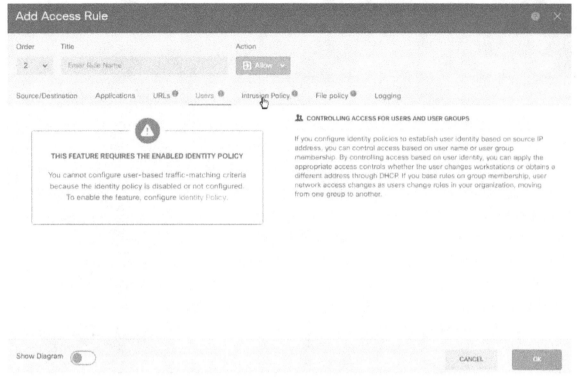

Granular control allows you to manage the user based access restrictions.

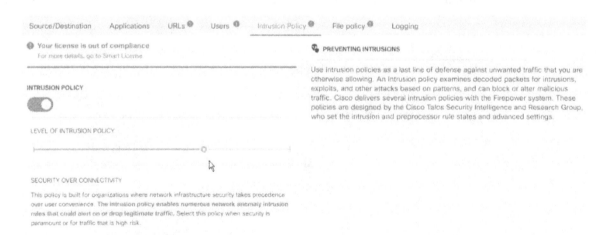

If you have any intrusion policy, specify it here unser Intrusion Policy tab. Note that these features requires advanced licenses.

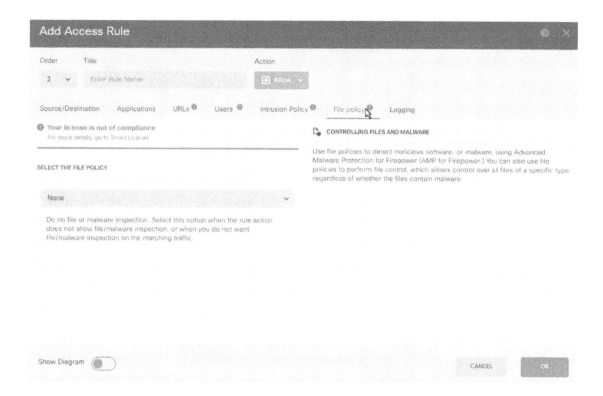

Optionally specify any file policy. For example if you wont want to allow .docx files, you can block it here.

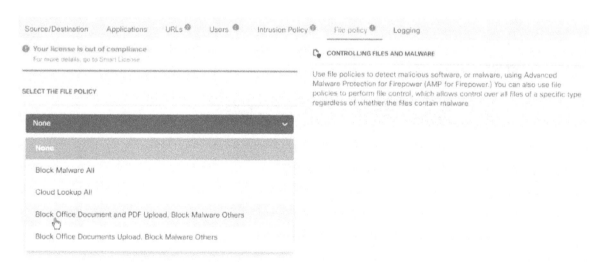

There are a few predefined policies and catagories. To update the contents of those predefines catagories, you need an internet connectivity. Also there is option for offline rule base update.

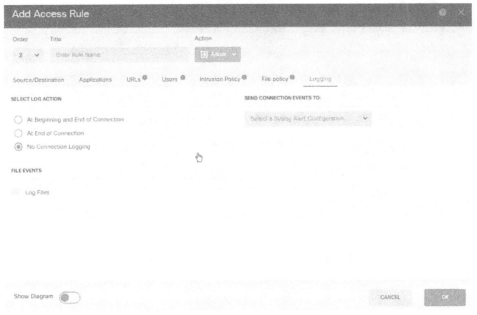

Enable logging from the logging tab. Click OK.

Now to add a NAT rule, go to the NAT tab. The configuration and concept is same , just the graphical interface is different.

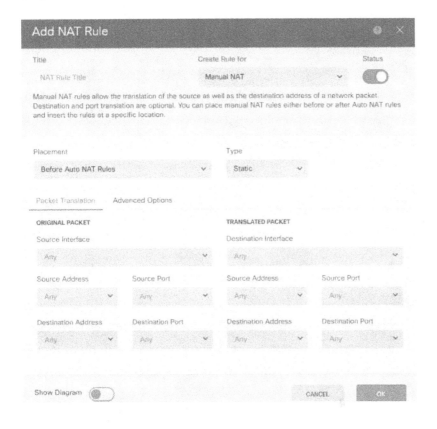

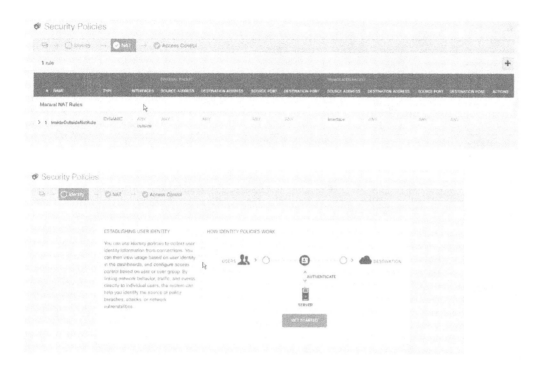

For enabling Identity security policy, you need to have connectivity with Cisco Identity services.

Under system settings, you can specify the management related settings such as logging, DHCP, NTP etc.

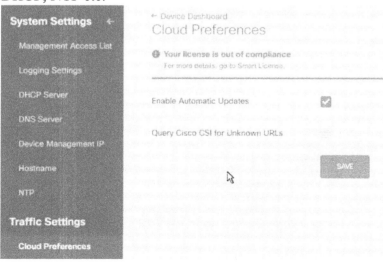

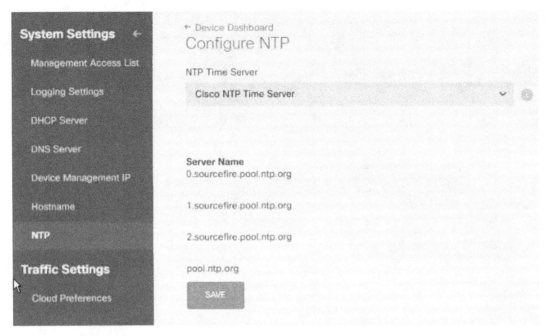

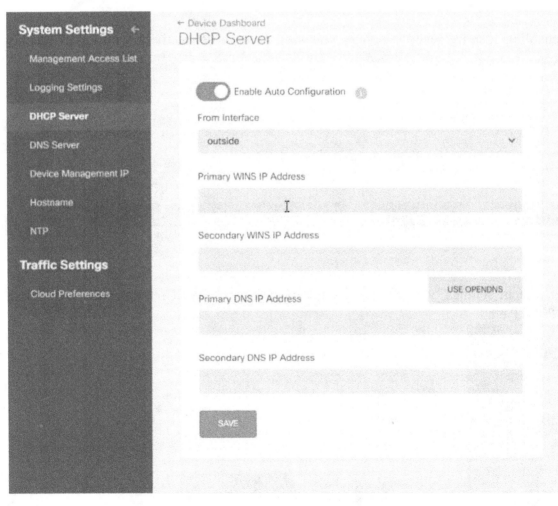

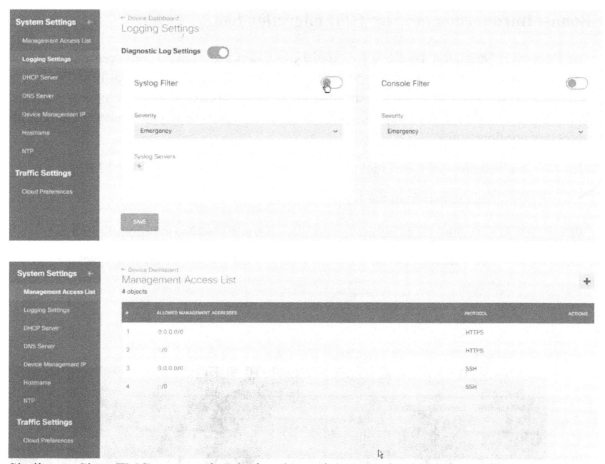

Similar on Cisco FMC, you need to deploy the settings to make things in to effect.

Summary

That is a brief introduction on Cisco FTD management using Firepower Device Management (FDM) web application. I didn't go in details on how to configuring each modules and concept. But I assume you already know the FTD management using FMC, then the local management using FDM should be pretty easy for you.

Bonus: Introduction to Cisco FTD migration tool.

The Firepower Migration Tool is a free tool from Cisco that converts the configuration of a supported ASA platform to a supported Firepower Threat Defense platform. With the Migration Tool, you can automate the migration of supported ASA features and policies. Well this tool is not a complete package for migration. But it helps you to convert almost all necessary configurations.

This tool is a web browser based tool and you much have connectivity to the FMC device.

You can download the tool from the following link,

https://www.cisco.com/c/en/us/products/security/firewalls/firepower-migration-tool.html

Once you download the tool, run it. This will load a small webserver on your machine.

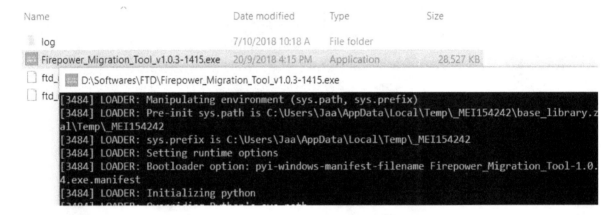

When the loading is finished, a webpage will automatically open up. That is actually the migration tool.

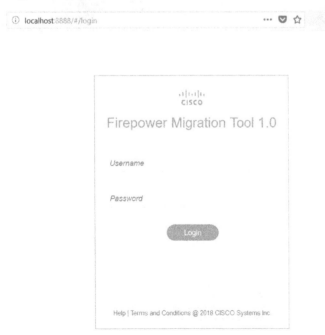

Login to the tool using the default credentials, username admin and password Admin123.

cisco Firepower Migration Tool

Pre-Migration Checklist

Before you begin your Adaptive Security Appliance (ASA) to Firepower Threat Defense migration, you must have the following items:

1. **Stable IP Connection:** Make sure that the Firepower Migration Tool has a stable connection to the Firepower Management Center throughout the migration process. Do not perform any changes on the Firepower Migration Center during the course of this migration.
2. **Firepower Management Center Version:** Make sure that the Firepower Management Center that manages the Firepower Threat Defense device is version 6.2.3 or above.
3. **Firepower Management Center Account:** Create a dedicated user account with administrative privileges for the Firepower Migration Tool and use those credentials during the migration.
4. **Firepower Threat Defense Device:** Add the target Firepower Threat Defense device to Firepower Management Center.
5. **ASA Configuration File:** Export a configuration file from a supported Adaptive Security Appliance (ASA) device in .cfg or .txt format.
6. **Default Browser:** Configure the system default browser as Google Chrome.

(New Migration)

It will show you a pre-migration checklist. Read it to understand and click on New Migration.

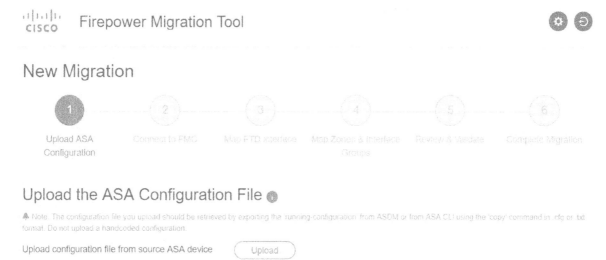

You can upload the configuration, convert it and apply it to the FMC. You can analyze the settings before deploying it in to the FTD device.

Summary

In this book, I have covered the configurations of FTD/FMC and management of FTD devices using the Cisco Firepower Management Centre (FMC). The topics I covered includes, setting up of the FTD and FMC devices from the scratch. Adding a FTD firewall in to the FMC. Configure the FTD firewall interfaces, Management settings, ACLs, NAT, Security policies, High Availability, etc. I have illustrated all the major concepts using a virtual lab.

Also I have explained step by step how to upgrade Cisco ASA to Cisco FTD and how to manage a standalone FTD device using the inbuilt Cisco Firepower Device Management. In the last section, I have given an introduction on FTD migration tool.

This book is intended mainly for the Network Security professionals and I encourage all the readers to setup and practice the lab thoroughly.

All the diagrams, IP addresses, numbers, names etc. used in this book is only for illustration purposes. They doesn't represent anything other than for examples and illustration. All the proprietary terms, reference links used here belongs to the respective owners.

I hope this book was informative to you and I wish all the best to you.

Note:

Check my other works on Amazon or follow my Author page **amazon.com/author/jithinalex**

Book	Description
NETWORK AUTOMATION USING PYTHON 3 — AN ADMINISTRATORS'S HANDBOOK EDITION 1, 2018 — JITHIN ABY ALEX	Network Automation using Python 3: An Administrator's Handbook Check and Buy on Amazon : **https://www.amazon.com/dp/B07HQZWKCG**
A COMPREHENSIVE GUIDE ON FIREWALL OPERATIONS AND BEST PRACTICES — BEING A FIREWALL ENGINEER — AN OPERATIONAL APPROACH FIRST EDITION, 2018 — JITHIN ABY ALEX	BEING A FIREWALL ENGINEER : AN OPERATIONAL APPROACH: A Comprehensive guide on firewall management operations and best practices Check and Buy on Amazon : **https://www.amazon.com/dp/B07HDJDG6R**

Check my articles, posts and opinions related to security, visit my personal blog **https://www.jaacostan.com**